"I have watched Kyle and Kelsey chase after God and I have seen His plans for them unfold like the most beautiful story. Now it's your turn! If you get one book for your daughter this year, get *The Chase*!"

—**Karen Kingsbury**, #1 *New York Times* bestselling author

"My friend Kelsey and her husband Kyle have written an inspiring and encouraging book about relationships called *The Chase*. Filled with stories from their own love story as well as their journey toward it, this book is informative and fun too! A must-read for single girls looking for a God-honoring relationship!"

—**Rebecca St. James**, Grammy and Dove Award–winning recording artist and author of *One Last Thing*

"Kyle and Kelsey have been friends of mine for several years. I love their passion for God, for family, and for young people. I believe this book will bring truth and light to readers and remind them of God's perfect plan for life."

—**Britt Nicole**, Grammy-nominated artist

"I'm so excited to read this book by my sweet friends Kelsey and Kyle. Their love story is beautiful, and their relationship is an inspiration of what it means to truly cherish each other!"

—**Francesca Battistelli**, Grammy-nominated Christian music superstar

"Kyle and Kelsey are a joy to know. They are genuine, sharp, fun-loving, and committed to chasing after God! They choose to live courageously in this generation. I encourage you to get to know them too through their inspiring story."

—**Pam Tebow**, speaker and mother of Tim Tebow

the
chase

the
chase

TRUSTING GOD *with* YOUR
happily ever after

KYLE *and* KELSEY
KUPECKY

Revell

a division of Baker Publishing Group
Grand Rapids, Michigan

Published by Revell
a division of Baker Publishing Group
P.O. Box 6287, Grand Rapids, MI 49516-6287
www.revellbooks.com

Printed in the United States of America

Library of Congress Cataloging-in-Publication Data
Kupecky, Kyle.
    The chase : trusting God with your happily ever after / Kyle and Kelsey
Kupecky.
        pages cm
    ISBN 978-0-8007-2651-5 (pbk.)
    1. Christian women—Religious life. 2. Christian life. 3. Marriage—
Religious aspects—Christianity. I. Title.
BV4527.K85 2015
248.4—dc23   2015017813

Scripture quotations labeled NLT are from the *Holy Bible*, New Living Translation, copyright © 1996, 2004, 2007 by Tyndale House Foundation. Used by permission of Tyndale House Publishers, Inc., Carol Stream, Illinois 60188. All rights reserved.

Scripture quotations labeled ESV are from The Holy Bible, English Standard Version® (ESV®), copyright © 2001 by Crossway, a publishing ministry of Good News Publishers. Used by permission. All rights reserved. ESV Text Edition: 2007

Scripture quotations labeled Message are from *The Message* by Eugene H. Peterson, copyright © 1993, 1994, 1995, 2000, 2001, 2002. Used by permission of NavPress Publishing Group. All rights reserved.

Scripture quotations labeled NIV are from the Holy Bible, New International Version®. NIV®. Copyright © 1973, 1978, 1984, 2011 by Biblica, Inc.™ Used by permission of Zondervan. All rights reserved worldwide. www.zondervan.com

Scripture quotations labeled NKJV are from the New King James Version. Copyright © 1982 by Thomas Nelson, Inc. Used by permission. All rights reserved.

Scripture quotations labeled VOICE are from The Voice Bible Copyright © 2012 Thomas Nelson, Inc. The Voice™ translation © 2012 Ecclesia Bible Society. All rights reserved.

Lyrics to "On the Inside" quoted in chapter 2 are written by Kyle Kupecky, Tyler Russell, and Brantley Pollock, Tunecore Songs o/b/o KBox Music (SESAC); Brantley Pollock Fair Trade Global Songs (BMI). Used by permission.

Wedding photos are by Jason Koenig/Studio JKoe. Used by permission.

The authors are represented by the literary agency of Alive Communications, Inc., 7680 Goddard Street, Suite 200, Colorado Springs, CO 80920, www.alivecommunications.com.

To protect the privacy of those who have shared their stories with the authors, some names and details have been changed.

15   16   17   18   19   20   21   7   6   5   4   3   2   1

To our precious child on the way . . .
You caught us by surprise, but we can't wait to hold you in
our arms and love you forever. Our prayer is that you will
chase after God all the days of your life. We can't wait to
meet you! We love you with our whole hearts.

----xo----

Contents

Foreword

by Karen Kingsbury

You picked up *The Chase* to learn a little about chasing God, about being in His will and finding your "happily ever after"—the one He has for your life. This book will speak straight to your heart. I believe that.

But when I see *The Chase* on the store shelves, it will always take me back.

Back to a sun-drenched Mexican beach, August 1, 1988.

It was the last day of our honeymoon, and my husband took my hand and smiled. "I have an idea," he said. He led me to the water, as close as we could get to the shore's edge. The blue sky stretched overhead, and we sat on the sand, side by side.

Donald turned to me, his eyes full of new love. "Let's pray for the family we might have. The kids God might give us, their spouses and children. Let's dedicate to the Lord all that might come after this moment."

Tears filled my eyes because I had just given my life to a man who truly chased after God and His Word and His plans not only for our lives but for the lives of our children. And so we linked hands and hearts and prayed. We asked for the Lord's blessing and direction, His wisdom and timing, His mercy and grace over our kids and their spouses and families.

However far off.

I can still feel the sun on my shoulders, still hear my husband's twentysomething voice mixing with the breeze off the ocean. The prayer is still fresh in my heart. It seemed all of heaven stood front row to the cries of our souls that day. That Mexican sand became holy ground. The thought even occurred to me, *We won't know until decades from now the power of this single prayer.*

Indeed.

Talk about chasing God.

We prayed when Kelsey was born, believing in the good plans God had for her. We prayed for her future impact on this world and for her future spouse. We prayed she would chase God the way we were still chasing Him. Kelsey's five brothers rounded out our family in the years to come, including three adopted from Haiti. We talked to God about all of our kids. Constantly. We still do.

Fast-forward to this moment.

Today, as you read *The Chase*, just know I'll be thinking about something more than that distant Mexican beach. As my daughter and son-in-love talk to you in this book about how they believe in chasing after God, I'll see myself sitting next to my husband praying in the shadow of Kelsey's crib, and I'll see us sitting on either side of her bed listening to her pray when she was two and four and the night before her first day of kindergarten. I'll see her heading out the door to middle school, and I'll remember begging God to keep her safe and protect her heart.

Right now you're holding *The Chase*, and you'll read a book full of possibility. But for me, I'll still see the summer sun glistening off the Columbia River in the Pacific Northwest on the evening of Kelsey's thirteenth birthday—the night she promised to chase God. And I'll remember holding her in my arms while she cried when she wasn't asked to a dance.

Because she was sticking to her promise: chasing God meant everything to her.

I'll be surrounded by memories of late-night talks with Kelsey when we agreed that she should pray for her future husband. Wherever he might be.

And I will remember being asked to attend a very special concert in Portland, Oregon. I will see Kelsey running down the stairs minutes before we left for that concert, changing her mind and deciding to attend the show.

And yes, I will see Kelsey in the catering room meeting Kyle Kupecky, the opening act for the Rock and Worship Roadshow. A young man chasing God . . . the way Kelsey was. I will remember the look in Kyle's eyes as they spoke, and I will recall thinking no one had ever looked at her that way before.

Finally, today when I see *The Chase* on a bookshelf, I will see Kyle Kupecky not as he looks on stage shining for Jesus at one of his concerts. I will see him standing at the front of the church, tears in his eyes, as our precious only daughter Kelsey walked down the aisle.

Yes. Kyle Kupecky was the one we had prayed for.

We were praying for Kyle when he was a second grader singing about Jesus in choir and on the fall of his thirteenth year when he wrote a letter to his future wife. Kyle was indeed the young man we had prayed for in the days before that concert in Portland. And all the way back to that sunny honeymoon beach and a prayer we prayed for our kids and their future spouses.

August 1, 1988.

I will remember that day, because it was on that day—at that very hour—that three thousand miles away, Kyle Kupecky was born.

Incredible, right? Chase God and you never know where He will take you!

I pray reading this book will be a life-changing experience for you. This may be the beginning of your chase or an encouragement to keep running the race. Either way, today as you read *The Chase*, you'll have something else to think about.

The beautiful story behind the book.

Karen Kingsbury
#1 *New York Times* bestselling author

Prologue

ONCE UPON A TIME

Once upon a time, in a land known as the West Coast, there lived a lovely young girl and her family. On her thirteenth birthday, the girl's parents took her out to dinner and presented her with a beautiful ring and a lovely journal.

The girl and her parents talked and prayed together about her future—and they prayed for the boy who would one day become the girl's husband. They encouraged her to read her Bible and write in her journal. Write down her thoughts, her hopes and dreams, and maybe even write a letter to her future husband.

After returning home that night, the girl knew she had to do one thing: write. Write down everything that had happened that day and write what was stirring deep within her soul. As she sat by the fireplace, she began writing in her brand-new journal. Thoughts swirled all around her. The girl wondered about her future. Dreamed about her future prince. Was he even real?

She listened to her parents' advice. The girl felt drawn to write a letter to her future husband. She had never done this before. After all, she didn't know who he was or where he was. But this night, on the pages of her new journal, she poured out her heart to him.

She told him she would be praying for him. She told him about the beautiful ring her parents had given her and the meaning behind it. She knew that life would be difficult and there would be temptations along the way; her parents warned her of that. But she told him that in God's strength she would save herself for him.

She signed it with X's and O's . . .

-----xo-----

Meanwhile, in a faraway land called the East Coast, a thirteen-year-old boy sat in a middle school youth group meeting where his leader proclaimed, "Somewhere out there is the girl you're going to marry. This is your chance to write to her, to let her know you're thinking of her and praying for her."

The leader passed out paper and pens to the group. When the boy received his paper, he looked out the window at the dark sky filled with bright stars. He thought about his future wife being out there somewhere—and wondered where she was and what she was doing.

The boy picked up the pen and began to write and pray for the girl who would someday become his wife. The boy longed to know this girl. When his letter was finished, the boy placed it in an envelope labeled "For My Future Wife."

And when he got home, he put the envelope in a wooden chest next to his bed for safekeeping.

————XO————

As the years went by, the boy and the girl grew, each in their separate lands. They thought often about the promises they had made and the love they had prayed for.

For the girl, her thirteenth and fourteenth years were full of happy friends and bright moments. Middle school quickly passed and high school years arrived. Years that were harder. She went to a large school where the pressure to look good, wear the right clothes, and act a certain way was sometimes unbearable.

Overall the years were lonely. Super lonely.

Sure, she had fun some of the time. She dated a few boys, but she never felt like her heart was safe. The guys she dated were respectful and nice, but she knew none of them was the guy she had been praying for.

As high school passed into college, the girl would often look at the ring her parents had given her and wonder whether she would ever find her Prince Charming—the guy who would really understand how to hold not only her hand . . . but her heart.

During her junior year of college the girl gave up on trying to make things happen with guys she knew she could never marry. She told God she was done with guys and just wanted to focus on her relationship with Him.

By now the boy had also grown up and had become a musician, singing for God onstage in front of thousands of people. He loved his job as a recording artist, but he was still waiting for God to answer his prayer for that one special girl.

And so it was the boy and girl found themselves in the same place at the same time one fine evening . . .

The boy rounded a corner backstage at one of his concerts and saw the girl standing next to a female security guard. The security guard was crying. The girl couldn't see the boy, but he was able to watch her. The boy took a few steps forward as the girl stood near the woman and prayed for her. The boy remained hidden from their view.

One thought ran through his mind as he watched: *I want my wife to have a heart like that.*

The thought surprised the boy. The trait was something he wanted for his future wife, of course. But never had he been so attracted to a girl's godliness. It gripped him now. Watching the girl comfort and give hope to a stranger captivated his heart in a way nothing ever had before.

In that moment his eyes were opened. Opened to a possibility. Opened to a chance. Opened to what just might be a one-in-a-million love.

----xo----

From the moment the boy and girl met later that evening, they were like lifelong friends. They made each other laugh, and they felt completely comfortable together. And of course they were also extremely attracted to each other. The details of their love story soon began to play out, constantly surprising them.

God had created them for each other—they were sure!

Before long, each was convinced that the other was the one they had been praying for all those years. Their lives of chasing God had led them to each other. The girl knew she couldn't live without the boy because he loved God and he understood her like no one else ever had. This boy filled her days with constant adventure.

And the boy knew this was the girl he wanted to marry. He could envision their wedding day. Their honeymoon. Kids playing in the front yard. A thousand beautiful seasons. Gray hair and wrinkled hands joined together.

Together, they knew this was a love God had been leading them to their whole lives.

----xo----

What happened from there? We'll share the details of our story with you later. We promise! But first we want you to know how very excited we are about *The Chase*. This book is about chasing after God in all aspects of life.

Sometimes it can be hard, and sometimes we get mixed up and chase after the wrong things. Our hope and prayer is that this book will encourage you to pursue God with all your heart.

We have one question for you: *Who are you chasing?*

Growing up, our parents and mentors used the Bible to guide us along a narrow path pointing us toward a future planned for us by God. That path shaped who we are today. And we hope this book—along with the Bible—will help guide you in that same way.

No, you aren't going to be perfect. None of us are. And you'll probably make some wrong steps along the way. But at the end of the day, always ask yourself, *Who or what am I chasing?*

Is it God?

If His name isn't your first answer, then you aren't headed in the right direction—His direction. God's been chasing after you since the day you were born. Are you chasing after Him? Is He your number one?

In the chapters ahead, you'll hear stories and advice from each of us individually as well as some things we'll share together as a couple. That way you can hear both a girl's and a guy's perspective on all of the topics we're about to cover.

> *Who are you chasing?*

Think of this book as a night spent hanging out with your best girlfriend talking about life and love and relationships, when suddenly there's a knock at the door and a guy walks in. In the chapters to come, he'll join in the conversation to give you the inside scoop on what a guy really thinks about love and relationships.

Ultimately, we want this book to inspire you to chase after the one person who really matters: Jesus Christ. He knows everything about you, and He loves you more than you know. He has the most amazing plans for you and desires a close personal relationship with you. God's dreams for you are out of this world. Keep chasing after Him, and you'll see.

> Trust GOD from the bottom of your heart;
>   don't try to figure out everything on your own.
> Listen for GOD's voice in everything you do,
>   everywhere you go;
> he's the one who will keep you on track.
>   Proverbs 3:5–6 Message

1

God First

When I was growing up, my parents always encouraged me to put God first in my life. They taught me to start the day with prayer and modeled what it looks like to set aside time for personal moments with God. They emphasized the importance of making my relationship with God the number one relationship in my life.

So why is it so hard to do that? I think it's because we have so many other things pulling at us and grabbing our attention. We are easily distracted, and being distracted prevents us from being productive. When we are distracted it's easier to keep our eyes focused on ourselves rather than on God.

If we really want to put God first in our lives, we must be willing to move some things around. If we find that our boyfriend is holding the number one spot in our lives rather than God . . . then it's time to do some shifting and rearranging.

----XO----

Putting God first before any dating relationship can be extremely difficult. My heart was made to love. I feel like God designed me that way. Of course I always want God to be first, but the problem is sometimes my dating relationships would get in the way of that.

Let me give you an example . . .

At the end of my sophomore year in college, I had a boyfriend I'd been dating for a little over a year. I really enjoyed his company (as did my family), and I definitely loved having a boyfriend. But I can't honestly say that I was in love with him. I mean, he was a nice guy and he loved the Lord, but there weren't complete sparks between the two of us.

Our relationship was safe, but it wasn't what I dreamed of.

The thing is, even though I knew he wasn't my Prince Charming, I still allowed our relationship to consume my brain and heart. Days were spent focused on him and our relationship, and basically he became my number one, which can happen so easily when you are in any kind of a dating relationship.

God would quite often take second place to my boyfriend.

Even though I knew my boyfriend wasn't really the right guy for me, I was way too stubborn to admit it out loud. When my mom would sweetly ask, "Kels, how are things with you guys?" I would typically smile and say, "They're great! He's so wonderful."

If we really want to *put God first* in our lives, we must be willing to *move some things around.*

My mom and I have always been extremely close, so she knew that wasn't entirely true, especially since I would choose to hang out with my brothers or friends over my boyfriend when given the option. But she didn't press the issue.

Throughout the second semester of that sophomore year, I had felt my boyfriend starting to pull away. Part of me didn't really blame him. We had first dated in high school, and it was fun having someone to go to dances with at the time. But now we were both in college and the next step wouldn't be going to the prom, it would most likely be marriage. Still, we continued to date each other.

On a Monday at the end of the school year, I was stressing out big-time about our upcoming biology final. My brain wasn't really best friends with biology. I was getting a C in the class, but I knew this final was going to be brutal and I couldn't afford to get a bad grade on it. My boyfriend was in the same class as me, so naturally we were studying all the time together for the final, which was approaching in two short days.

So while I was beyond stressed about the final, at least I knew I would have the support and help of my boyfriend. We studied long and hard that week, but the day before our exam something happened that rocked my world. (Sounds dramatic, right? Let me assure you, it was!)

My boyfriend broke up with me.

I was sitting in the library waiting for him to come study, when I looked down at my phone and saw his text pop up on my screen: "Kels, we need to talk. Please meet me outside on our bench."

My heart completely stopped. My boyfriend had just texted me those famous last words, "We need to talk." And he wanted me to meet him at *our* bench. The bench where we would take our coffee between classes and laugh and talk. I know I told you this guy wasn't my Prince Charming, but he was still my boyfriend of a very long time and I cared about him.

With a feeling of dread, I took a deep breath, gathered up my things, and headed outside. I could see him sitting at our bench about a hundred yards away. His shoulders were slumped and his head was bent as he stared at the ground.

Is this actually happening? was all I could think as I walked toward him.

Over the course of the next hour, my soon-to-be-ex-boyfriend explained how he could tell that I didn't really love him and that he knew I wasn't as into the relationship as he was. I started to cry because everything he was saying was true.

I had lost myself in just wanting to have and keep a boyfriend. I had let our relationship become number one in my life over God.

We had a long hug goodbye, and before he turned away he said, "I'll always be here for you, Kels. Oh, and good luck tomorrow on our final."

The next morning I woke up, went to look in the mirror, and could barely see my eyes. They were swollen shut because the night before I had cried my heart out.

Heartbreak is horrible. Breaking up is the worst.

Even when you know deep down that it probably is the right thing, it doesn't change the fact that your heart is shattered. Oh, and to top it all off, I had to go see my now ex-boyfriend and take my biology final.

This was *not* my best day.

My ex-boyfriend and I didn't see much of each other at all after that. It was too hard. Later that summer, I was sitting outside by myself just thinking. I knew I had let my boyfriend replace God as being first in my life. I had stopped chasing what mattered most. It was so clear to me once I was out of the relationship.

Now, it's not necessarily bad to date. It's not necessarily bad to have a boyfriend whom you love with all of your heart. But we always need to ask ourselves, What are we chasing? Who are we chasing? We need to always keep God first in our hearts and in our lives. When we let boys and dating become our number one priority, we wind up feeling confused and empty.

Dating or having a serious relationship is wonderful if you are with the right kind of godly person. God never says dating is bad. But when that person becomes more important than God . . . that's when you should rethink the relationship. That's when you need to refocus and make God the number one priority in your life again.

When I met Kyle, I could tell he was different from any other guy I had met before. The way he treated others and his humble spirit spoke volumes about his character. Kyle is not perfect (although he is pretty close, if you ask me). I'm not perfect. But I can tell you that when we met each other, we were both putting God first in our lives.

I'm not saying we had all the answers, because we most certainly did not. But we had each made a strong and bold decision to follow after Jesus and to put God first. Also, I have to tell you that both of us were completely happy and content with being single at the time. I was in a place where I was done with dating, and Kyle was in that place too.

We wanted God to be first in our lives. We still want that.

----xo----

When my parents encouraged me to chase after God first in my life, they weren't demanding I be perfect. God knows everything about us. He knows we aren't going to be perfect. And guess what? He loves us just the same!

But my parents did offer me and my brothers beautiful advice when they encouraged us to put God first. God's plans are better than our own. His ways are beyond our comprehension. Even when we can't understand something that we are going through or a situation a friend is in . . . God does.

He knows best.

God doesn't want to be number one in your life because He is a selfish God. Definitely not. Rather, He wants to be number one in your life because He loves you that much. He sent His Son, Jesus, down to earth to die on a cross for all of your sins and for all of mine.

God loves us so much that when we mess up, He is right there with an ocean of grace, waiting for us to return to Him. When we put God first in our lives, we end up worrying less and we have an internal peace that we can't really explain.

I'm not suggesting that when you repent of your sins and fol-low God your life will be perfect. That's not the case. But God's

God's plans are always far better than our own.

plans are always far better than our own. We all have plans and dreams for our lives, but trust me, God's plans will end up being the *best* plans and dreams possible.

27

Putting God first is not always easy, and it's true that we can all get highly distracted with work, friendships, and dating relationships. But through it all, keep putting God first.

-----XO-----

Do you put God first in your life? How often do you read your Bible? When was the last time you read it—not so that you could check it off your Christian to-do list, but because you actually wanted to dive into God's Word?

I can get super busy, and sometimes a week (or even more) goes by, and I haven't stopped all of the craziness around me and picked up my Bible. God is there waiting for you and me to run to Him. Reading the Bible regularly is a great way to put God first.

Another fun way to put God first is to journal your prayers and thoughts. If you are like me, you probably have a million questions, emotions, and thoughts running through your brain. Try writing down some of those thoughts and prayers. I find that when I'm reading my Bible and also journaling my prayer requests, I feel closer to God.

From Kyle

I failed miserably at chasing God while I dated my first girlfriend. I was right out of high school and eager to have a girlfriend. There were no Christian prospects at my high school, so college was an amazing opportunity for love.

I started dating the first girl I met. I didn't care who the girl was, I just really wanted a girlfriend. What a jerk move. I wish I could go back in time and punch the old me in the face, then tell the girl to run for the hills and stay away from that guy because he's only going to break your heart.

As this girl and I started dating, I could tell early on that I wasn't as into her as she was into me. But I kept the relationship going because it was nice to have someone, even if I knew there was no real future with her. I pushed aside any feelings of guilt for leading her on.

I was too wrapped up in having a girlfriend. I wasn't protecting her heart. I was protecting my relationship status.

I was spending lots of time with friends and with my girlfriend but not tons of time with God. I had barely even prayed about this relationship. I was not putting God first in my life, and it really showed.

There was another girl on campus who I started developing feelings for, but I knew I couldn't pursue her while I still had a girlfriend. So I dumped my first girlfriend via text message. Not at dinner, not even over the phone, but by *text message*.

Again, a complete jerk move.

I so wish I could go back and end that relationship differently. I would apologize for being so selfish. I wasn't putting her first and I wasn't putting God first. I was putting Kyle first.

The secret to being ready for a relationship is keeping your heart connected to God.

> *None of us are ready for a romantic relationship until we chase God first.*

None of us are ready for a romantic relationship until we chase God first. Until we pursue Him with our whole heart. That way, you'll be defined by

God's love. Not by a guy. Your beauty and self-worth will be wrapped up in God, bringing you peace and confidence.

If you keep yor heart connected to God, you'll certainly be ready for whatever or whoever comes your way.

----XO----

A high school friend of mine chased after God in a way I'll never forget.

. Brody was the star of the football team. He was only a sophomore, but his talent on the field rivaled that of any senior. He was a team player, a great leader, and also a Christian. Colleges had begun to take notice of him, and so had some of the senior cheerleaders.

It was known around campus that Brody was a Christian. But what really had people talking was the fact that he was a self-professed virgin. Brody had told a friend that he was going to wait for sex until he was married. That news spread around the school like wildfire. And some of the cheerleaders wanted to see just how far Brody *would* go.

After practice one day, Brody pushed open the locker room door to leave and nearly crashed into Shelby, the captain of the cheer squad.

"Oh, sorry!" Brody said, grabbing Shelby's arm so she wouldn't fall.

"Why, thank you!" Shelby gasped as she rested her hand on Brody's bicep. "You're Brody," she whispered with a smile, "aren't you?"

Brody had lowered his hand to his side, but Shelby kept her hand firmly on his bicep.

"Yeah, that's me," Brody replied.

Shelby lowered her eyes and looked slowly back up at Brody.

"Good," she said through a slight smile. "I wanted to meet you. Bump into me anytime."

She squeezed his bicep, slowly let her hand roll down his arm, and then turned and walked away. Brody was left breathless. Shelby had left quite the impression.

When Brody arrived at school the next day, something had changed. Immediately, some of the guys from his team ran down the hall to greet him.

"Dude, Shelby? No way!" one guy yelled.

"Bro, she wants you," another said, punching Brody's side.

"What?" Brody asked, dumbfounded. "What are you guys talking about?"

Derek, Brody's co-captain on the team, stepped forward from the crowd of guys circling Brody. "Look at this, bro."

Derek held up his phone to Brody's face. Brody read the Twitter post on the top of the screen. It was from Shelby's account. The post read, "I think it's time that football player scores some points off the field . . . He's HOT."

Derek laughed. "Dude, that's you!"

Brody was shocked. The blood drained from his face in less than a second.

"You're gonna get some!" Derek pushed one of Brody's shoulders.

"Guys, I'm not about that," Brody shot back. "You know me," he said loud enough for the whole group to hear. "You know what I believe. This doesn't change that."

"You've *got* to be kidding me!" Derek almost screamed. "The hottest girl at our school wants to hook up with you . . . and you're gonna say *no*?"

"Yeah," Brody spoke confidently. "I'm gonna say no."

The group began to laugh, some almost falling over in disbelief. Brody stood his ground, trying not to let the laughter of his so-called friends get to him. After a painful ten seconds, the laughter died down and Derek turned to walk away. The group followed his lead.

As he slid away, Derek yelled out one more comment: "Whatever, Brody . . . I guess you're gayer than I thought."

The group howled in laughter as they made their way down the hall. Brody was angry. He stood in the hallway fighting back tears. It was the worst day of his high school career.

That night Brody went to his church's high school youth group. He was emotionally exhausted, and it was obvious to some of his close friends that something was up. These youth group friends were very different from Brody's friends at school.

His school friends played sports and were fun to hang out with, but they didn't have the same beliefs he did. Brody would go to school, study hard, play sports, and have a good time with his school friends, but the guys who really understood him were these guys in youth group who huddled up around him now.

"Brody, what's up, man?" one of the guys asked.

"I feel like I'm falling and failing." The words just fell out of his mouth. Quickly he explained the entire story to the guys around him. Bumping into Shelby. The tweet she posted. The encounter with Derek and the rest of the football team that day.

"I'm trying to do the right thing here," Brody wrestled out. "I truly want to please God. Obviously, I know having sex with Shelby would not please Him. But now everyone at my school thinks I'm a joke." Brody sighed. "They'll never respect me again."

"Wow," said Thomas, Brody's closest friend at youth group. "That's some insane pressure." He leaned closer and said, "But you stood up to it. You didn't let it break you. You didn't cave."

"Thanks, man," Brody said with a hint of a smile.

"No, seriously!" Thomas proclaimed. "You were true to what you believe with *all* those guys right in your face. That right there is legit. God is going to bless you for that." Thomas stood up and motioned for the other guys to stand. "Let's all pray for Brody right now. That whatever he faces tomorrow, God will give him the strength to endure and be strong."

He looked right at Brody and said, "You can do this. People respect courage. People respect someone standing firm on what they believe. The football guys will come around eventually. Be strong, bro."

The guys came around Brody and began to pray for him. Brody could feel his spirit encouraged. It was like life and strength were being poured back into him. He was ready for tomorrow.

Tomorrow came and it wasn't any easier.

Brody walked down the hall and could hear the guys on the team laughing at him. But Brody didn't let it hurt him deeply like he had the day before. God was taking the hits for him. That's what he envisioned in his mind every time someone made fun of him.

He saw Shelby in the hall, but when he passed her he would just ignore her obvious advances. If anything, her desperate attitude was unattractive to Brody. He felt sorry for her.

By lunchtime, it seemed as if the jokes from the guys had toned down a bit. They had tried to get to him, but Brody wouldn't allow them to get under his skin. Maybe his cool and collected attitude had diminished their aggression. Or so he thought.

At lunchtime, Derek made his way over to Brody's table and sat directly across from him. If anyone truly had hurt Brody, it was Derek. And by the look on Derek's face as he sat down, it was clear that lunch was about to turn ugly.

"So, you're not gonna do it?" Derek shot at Brody.

"Dude, what is your problem?" Brody asked.

"Oh, I don't have a problem," Derek replied with surprise. "But I think *you* do. I don't get you, man."

"Well, I'm sorry you don't 'get' me," Brody replied.

"Just do it, dude," Derek said sternly. "Everyone thinks you're a joke. I'm trying to look out for you."

By now the entire lunch table had quieted and everyone's attention had turned to Brody and Derek.

"You're right," Brody said. Derek's eyebrows shot up. "I could hook up with her." He waited a beat and added, "I could be just like you."

A tension filled the air between Brody and Derek. All eyes and ears were glued on what Brody would say next.

"But you could never be just like me."

I was one of the guys in Brody's youth group, and his story has always stayed with me. His determination to put God first in his life has been a huge example to me. Brody's high school experience didn't magically get easier or better because he did the right thing. But in time, the guys eventually backed off him. And his firm stance gained back the respect of many. Brody was a born leader on and off the field. But more importantly, he let God lead his life. He put God first even when it cost him.

- - - - -xo- - - - -

When I was younger, people would tell me, "Oh, just wait. Right now work on waiting." To me, waiting sounds very passive. Like I'm sitting on a couch with my hands tied. There's no action to it.

That kind of advice is only half of the solution. Better advice is to wait *and* chase God. While you're waiting for the love of your life, pursue God.

In my sophomore year of college I did just that. I was studying music at a Christian school, Liberty University, when an opportunity hit me in the face. A Christian pop group was forming, and they wanted me to be a part of it.

Music and singing had always been my passion, and this opportunity would allow me to use the gifts God had given me to make an impact in the world for Him. I knew with everything inside me that this group was what I was supposed to do. I signed on and things quickly took off.

I found myself living in Nashville and recording an album, all the while being single. It was a year and a half of adventure, new beginnings, and lots and lots of prayer. We landed our first stadium tour, and I couldn't believe it!

The tour was crazy. Five different cities in one week. Sleeping on a bus. Living out of a suitcase. Always on the go.

But on March 8, time froze.

Everything stood still when I was introduced to a girl backstage. Her name was Kelsey.

Never in my wildest dreams did I think I was going to meet my future wife that night. I was halfway across the country from home in a state I had never visited before. At the same time, it completely makes sense that I met Kelsey then.

I was letting God lead my heart. I had been single for a while. It was the perfect moment to meet Kelsey, and it happened while I was chasing after God.

In Matthew 22:37 Jesus says, "Love the Lord your God with all your heart, all your soul, and all your mind." We are called to love God with *everything* and to put Him first above *anything* else.

> *On March 8, time froze. Everything stood still when I was introduced to a girl backstage. Her name was Kelsey.*

Before I met Kelsey, I had been single for a year and a half. No flings, no almost relationships . . . *single*. In that time I was focused on where God was leading me. It was clear that this was a time for me to be single and pursue God with everything I had.

It was a growing time.

A time for me to transition from a passionate boy to a godly man.

There is absolutely no way I would have been ready to lead Kelsey if I had not had that year and a half of alone time. I had to get to the place where God was enough for me. Where I didn't need to have a romantic relationship in my life.

Think of being single as a time when God is preparing you for your future. Every minute, every hour, every month, every year of singleness is a crucial part of your preparation and journey to meet your potential future love.

I longed for Kelsey while I was single.

Of course, at the time I didn't know my future wife would be Kelsey, but I longed for that best friend and true love. I went to God with my longing. I talked to Him about her. I prayed for her—that God would keep her safe, that God would bless her dreams, that God would protect her family, and that I would be the man she needed me to be when I finally met her.

She was constantly on my mind, and it was beautiful. It wasn't a constant thought of "I need to find my wife!" It was more an attitude of "I can't wait to be with her . . . God, I trust You to work out the when and where."

> Seek the Kingdom of God above all else . . . and he will give you everything you need. (Matt. 6:33 NLT)

From Us Both

How about you? What is the one thing or person that is taking the place of God in your life? Who are you chasing after? Maybe it's time to rearrange, refocus, and start putting God first again.

God is right there waiting for you. Let the chase begin!

2

Quiet the Noise

Why is it that the world is so loud?

This is a question I ask myself quite often. I'm not saying the world is an awful place, but it can be so loud. Our minds get cluttered with popular culture, fashion, music, movies, TV, magazines, friends, social media, celebrities . . . the list goes on and on.

Sometimes it can be hard to really hear the truth. With so many products and people shouting at us to go a certain direction or be a certain way, truth can sometimes get lost in the mix of all the chaos and noise.

My parents taught me to believe that I am a princess, a one-in-a-million girl. Not in an arrogant way but in a way that breathed hope and life into my heart. They told me that my beauty comes from within. It comes from Jesus. I love this idea! Because guess what? It couldn't be more true.

Sometimes it's easy to forget that truth, though. Especially when we start listening to all the noise in the world around us. All of us (including me) tend to look to other people when it comes to our self-worth or our beauty. But where we really need to be looking is Jesus. He made each of us in our own special and beautiful way.

You are a one-in-a-million girl. Do you believe it?

The world tells us that beauty is the most important thing. We get that message from celebrities, the media, and even from our own minds. But when you stop and think about it, is beauty really the most important thing? Should it be the most important thing? Let those questions really sink into your heart.

It's so easy and completely normal to notice someone's outer appearance at first, but I want to encourage you to go a lot further than just outer beauty. Every person you come into contact with has a story. Every person has goals, hopes, and dreams somewhere inside their heart. If we only notice a person's outward appearance, then we miss who they really are. We miss what's on the inside, who they are as a person and what's in their heart.

A few months ago I was in the airport headed back home and grabbed a magazine for the plane ride. I opened up to the table of contents, and what I found wasn't really a surprise, it just made me a little sad. I absolutely *love* fashion, hair, make-up, and basically anything girly. I also love reading

If we only notice a person's outward *appearance,* then we miss **who they really are.**

magazines about those things, but sometimes the articles hit me in a sad way.

This was one of those times. Nine out of ten articles featured in the magazine were about looks, dieting, chasing youthful beauty, and becoming a more beautiful you (on the outside). Again, I wasn't too surprised. I enjoy talking about and reading articles on eating healthy, working out, fashion, and style. There is absolutely nothing wrong with taking care of yourself and wanting to be beautiful. However, it must be done in a healthy way, and it shouldn't be your all-consuming thought every single day.

Magazines and TV send a very different message about inner beauty, though, and it's a troubling one. If I had to sum up the message our culture sends us, it would be this:

- Inner beauty doesn't catch anyone's eye!
- Character doesn't matter. Confidence does.
- If you're not perfect looking, you should at least be trying.

No joke! I see this message shouted at you and me every time I turn on the TV or scroll through social media on my phone. As if inner beauty is old-fashioned, a thing of the past.

We all know that since the beginning of time people have wanted to be beautiful. It's not something that's suddenly become all the rage. But to think that inner beauty should be thrown out the window and all we should care about is our outer appearance . . . that hurts my heart.

I was flipping through a magazine recently and noticed how celebrities were featured talking about diets that helped them stay thin or products that helped them look young and beautiful. In some ways the articles were interesting. Like I mentioned, I love having recommendations for what to put on my skin and what type of healthy foods I should be eating. I just don't want to become so obsessed with other people's pursuit of external perfection that I lose sight of my own thoughts or, even worse, God's thoughts.

Our bodies really aren't our own. They belong to God. And because He made each of us uniquely beautiful, we should want to take care of our bodies and appreciate them. So it's important to quiet the celebrities we admire and the magazines we like to read and listen to what God has to say.

Isn't it funny how people can shout from the rooftops about someone or something that changed their life, but when someone mentions God, people get completely freaked out and awkward? This makes me upset. Shouldn't God's voice be the loudest? I don't say that just because it's the right thing to say . . . I really mean it. Shouldn't we all live our lives worrying about what God thinks of us rather than what the world thinks?

To be honest, if the articles I read that day had mentioned God, they would've all made more sense. We can't simply wish to be thin, to stay healthy, or to have a better daily routine. Our minds are powerful, yes. So wishing or hoping for something might work for a while, but eventually we will run out of ways to motivate ourselves.

That's when the Lord steps in and reminds us that He's there. He's always there, patiently waiting for us to run to Him. God knows what's on your heart, and He definitely knows if you have thoughts of being healthier, prettier, skinnier . . . maybe your list goes on and on.

Give all of your worries and all of your anxieties over to God. By doing so you will be able to hear His voice louder than all the other voices. You will be able to quiet the noise, even if just for a little while.

----xo----

Celebrities and fashion magazines aren't the only voices in our lives that can distract us from God's perspective. Sometimes it's our friends who are creating the most noise.

I was in the lunchroom during a very normal week of high school. Our lunch period was only thirty minutes, so it always felt like a whirlwind. I sat down at a table with some of my friends, both guys and girls.

The guys at the table were talking loudly and unabashedly about girls, how "this one is hot" or "that one is easy." I was already annoyed. Wouldn't they be a little upset if we girls sat down and immediately started talking loudly about other guys and how hot they were? I mean, come on!

The guys wouldn't quit, though. They kept going on and on about hot girls at our school, and then they moved on to hot girls in general. My friends and I rolled our eyes and tried to talk about something else. I asked my friend Mackenzie if she had a lot of homework, and some other non-dramatic questions were thrown around our lunch table. But the guys quickly turned the conversation back to girls and who they were thinking about taking to the neon dance.

The neon dance was one of the most fun dances my school put on. It was crazy. Everyone showed up decked out in as much neon as they could possibly find.

I was excited for the dance, but there was one slight problem: I needed to find a date. As the guys continued talking about different girls, my mind started racing.

Maybe I should've worn a different outfit today. Maybe if I hung out more with these guys outside of school they would be talking about me. Did I wear enough make-up today? What in the world is my hair doing right now?

So many doubts and questions started to cloud my mind. Then the bell rang and it was time to head back to class.

I remember feeling stupid and insecure as I walked to class. *My guy friends didn't think I was hot, or else they would've talked about me at lunch, right?* I was almost to my next class. *Or maybe they do think I'm hot, but they obviously couldn't say that with me right there! One of the guys will surely ask me to the dance . . . right?* I was paranoid with questions.

Our school hired a real DJ from our local Top 40 radio station. Everyone was pumped. Even my teacher opened up our class with, "The neon dance sounds like it's going to be the best dance of the year. We had a brief teachers meeting this morning, and the principal mentioned it. Sounds awesome. Not that much time left to find a date! Anyway, get out your books and turn to page 56 . . ."

Are you kidding me? It felt like I was in the middle of some nightmare. But when the bell rang at the end of the period, I realized that, nope, I was wide awake. And this was my reality. I still didn't have a date.

Suddenly my brain felt cluttered and weighed down by negative thoughts. I was obsessing over the neon dance. A thousand insecurities flashed through my head. I was consumed with noise and nonsense. I was spiraling into negativity. Thankfully, that's when it hit me. I needed to pause . . . take a breath . . . and pray.

You see, praying doesn't have to be fancy or perfectly planned out. Praying is just telling God what's on your heart, letting Him know how you are feeling, why you are frustrated, or why you are happy.

Right there in the hall, as I headed for my next class, that's exactly what I did. I prayed silently in my heart that God would give me clarity and truth.

> *Praying doesn't have to be fancy or perfectly planned out. Praying is just telling God what's on your heart.*

I prayed I would see myself the way He sees me, which is beautiful. All of a sudden this confidence and calmness that I can't really explain washed over me. My head hurt less, and the people and things around me became quiet. Ahhh . . . peace.

God is always with us, and He cares so deeply for us. I should've prayed right there at the lunch table when I started feeling not good enough and not pretty enough. Sometimes the voices from friends and guys we know, whether they go to our school or our church, can be louder than God's voice.

Don't let that be the case. God wants to give us peace and truth. Make His voice the loudest in your life.

----xo----

Another voice that seriously distracts me is the voice of social media. Even though we all love Facebook, Twitter, Instagram, YouTube, and other social media outlets, they can become an all-consuming thing. Maybe you've experienced that. I don't even want to know how many total hours I've spent on those apps and websites. It would be embarrassing because I know it's *way* too many.

I use Facebook to keep in touch with my personal friends from my childhood and also my current friends. I use Twitter to keep in touch with all of you. And I mainly use Instagram for pictures of Kyle and me . . . no shame there. I love You-Tube for humorous skits and videos. My brothers and I look up funny stuff on YouTube all the time.

But even though these social media outlets bring me joy, I know that I probably spend way too much time on them. And that can create some problems.

During my sophomore year in college, I was studying theater, I didn't have a boyfriend, and I was away from home. This meant that after class I had plenty of downtime to catch up on . . . you guessed it, social media!

It sounds funny, but it's what we all do, right? If you're like me, then your phone is probably always with you. That makes checking what's going down on the internet so much easier.

After class I would immediately grab my phone out of my backpack and start reading up on what I missed. It became a constant habit for me. I would search for ex-boyfriends and see what other friends were doing.

I found myself comparing my life to other people's lives. I would look at people's profiles and think, *Wow, they have so many friends! Or, Man, everyone is dating someone. Even my ex-boyfriend has someone. I'm so single.*

Social media was totally bringing me down.

That semester I had memorized and performed dozens of monologues, was in several dance classes every single week, and met with my voice teacher twice a week. Sometimes we forget how blessed our real life is and we start living for our online profile.

That's exactly what I was doing. Not only was I trying to keep up with everyone around me, but I was still comparing myself and feeling like I didn't measure up.

In the busyness of the semester, I noticed that my quiet time with God was sort of nonexistent. Reading my Bible and talking to God were happening less and less. I loved God more than anyone or anything, but somehow I became too busy to talk to Him. However, I was never too busy to call my family or Skype with my mom or—here's the real kicker—be on social media.

I was in need of some boundaries when it came to social media.

I needed to spend some time with the Lord—reading my Bible, praying, singing worship songs—before spending time online. I have to tell you that although it was hard at first, it quickly became easier. Once I had it in my mind that I would talk to God first and then check social media, I really felt closer to God and much happier.

If you are feeling like you need a break from social media, then take one. It doesn't make you weird at all. In fact, it will probably allow you to breathe and get refocused on God. It certainly did for me.

----xo----

Quiet the noise. That's one of my favorite phrases. God wants us to be still, to wait upon Him and His timing for our lives. It's so hard to truly hear God's voice when we are letting celebrities, TV, friends, guys, and social media tell us what to do and who to be.

Stop comparing yourself to other people.

Please make God's voice the loudest in your life. You will never, ever regret it. When we slow down and shut off all the other voices, that's when Jesus really becomes the most important voice in our heads and in our hearts. Listen to the voice of truth.

You are beautiful. And you are God's greatest treasure.

From Kyle

Have you ever gone to camp or maybe been on a family vacation where you had to leave your cell phone, computer, and TV behind? A time where you were truly off the grid. Do you remember how it felt?

I know those times for me have felt freeing. I've had some of my richest moments with God when I've unplugged from the world and turned all of my attention to Him. Clarity comes when we quiet the noise.

Our generation battles the loudest noise and most distractions of any generation that has walked this planet. We can access billions of pages of information with the touch of a button. We have endless hours of music to listen to and millions of movies to watch. And even though we may not realize it, all this information and entertainment influences our hearts.

> *Clarity comes when we quiet the noise.*

When I was in high school, I loved having TV parties with my friends. We would go to someone's house and watch one of our favorite shows together. One show in particular focused on a group of high schoolers and the drama that surrounded their lives in sunny California. My friends and I loved it. It had dramatic storytelling, a great soundtrack, and good actors. It also had quite a bit of romance. And as with most teen dramas on TV, that came with a good deal of sexual situations.

They didn't show actual sex on TV, but they sure pushed that boundary. I knew deep down that it wasn't good for me to watch, but the story pulled me in. And all my friends loved it. I told myself that the bad scenes weren't affecting me. I knew those things went against God's Word, so I just wouldn't focus on them. Since all my friends watched this show, I thought it would be extreme to not watch it just because of a few scenes here and there.

Little did I know how much this show *was* affecting me.

There was a girl in my class at that time who was very beautiful. We both knew we liked each other, and there was definite chemistry between us. Unfortunately, this girl wasn't a Christian. She knew I was, though, and that I had said I wouldn't date a non-Christian.

I was proud of my faith, and my friends knew what I believed. From talking to my parents and reading the Bible, I knew that if I dated someone who didn't believe what I did . . . well, then my faith could be at risk. My belief in God would surely take a hit if I pursued a relationship with someone who didn't love Jesus.

But the attraction with this girl was still there, and I didn't want to ignore it. So I convinced myself that kissing her once in a while would be okay. I knew I wasn't going to actually date her, because I only wanted to date someone who loved

Jesus. But a kiss here and there . . . I told myself that it would be fine. So that's what we did.

Looking back, my faith must have been laughable to this girl. Yes, I told her about Jesus and even invited her to church. But where were my convictions? I told her I would only date a Christian, but then I showed her I was perfectly fine doing things that only a committed couple should do. It must have been very confusing for her. My actions weren't representing my faith well.

I should have told her I love God, I want to follow His plans for my life, and I'm going to save my affections for someone who also loves Jesus. She probably would have made fun of me, but I'm sure that would have made her wonder about my faith and respect it more.

Unfortunately, I let the subtle messages of a TV show speak into my life more than the truth of God's Word. Week by week I was watching casual relationships play out on TV, and guess what? I ended up in a casual relationship with a girl who wasn't a Christian.

Yes, the TV show was affecting me.

The noise around you right now (maybe a TV show?) might make

> Big mistakes don't just happen. They start off as one little compromise after another.

you compromise . . . just a little. And that's all it takes to set you off course. Big mistakes don't just happen. They start off as one little compromise after another.

----xo----

When Jesus walked this earth, the Bible tells us, He routinely got away from the city and would hike up a mountain to be alone with the Father. He went off to the desert for forty days to pray and spend time alone with God. He got away from the distractions and quieted the noise.

> Before daybreak the next morning, Jesus got up and went to an isolated place to pray. (Mark 1:35)

Are you seeing the pattern here?

Jesus leads by example. He needed time alone with God to recharge and to see what God had for Him. If Jesus, the supernatural Son of God, needed time alone with His Father, how much more do we need time alone with God?

Taking bold steps to protect yourself from the strong pulls of this world is a large task, but it can be done. God's promise to help us and strengthen us is real.

But if we don't go to Him for supernatural strength, we won't get it.

Be careful of how much "stuff" you let inside your life. Not all of it is beneficial. Most things will distract us from God. When we quiet the noise around us, only then will we be able to truly hear Him.

> So faith comes from hearing, that is, hearing the Good News about Christ. (Rom. 10:17)

-----XO-----

As a recording artist, I pray the songs I write will speak to listeners' hearts and draw them closer to God. Fan letters always encourage me, and some of the stories in them blow me away. Especially those from girls like Amber . . .

For most of middle school, Amber was the girl in the background. She never stood out, but she also never went out of her way to hide. She just blended in naturally. Maybe it was her personality, or maybe it was her face. Whatever the case, she felt pretty forgettable.

Amber would get invited to some parties, but not nearly as many as Chloe Walker did. Chloe and her friends were skinny, blonde, pretty, and the four most popular girls in Amber's eighth-grade class. They acted like they were already in high school. Everyone looked at them. Talked about them. Wanted to be like them. Including Amber.

These girls weren't nice, but Amber still looked up to them. Most days she wanted to be just like them. So as her eighth-grade year began, she knew one thing: she would be one of them. It might take some time, but she was determined to be liked and popular.

Since the girls would never even give Amber the time of day, she decided to study them online. She could only stare from a distance in person, but she could see all the intimate details of their lives from their Instagram, Twitter, and Snapchat accounts. None of the girls kept their accounts private because they wanted the most likes and followers.

As Amber followed the girls online, she became obsessed. After school she would rush home, finish her homework, and then start her real "homework." She spent hours studying them. She would check to see what the girls were talking about, buying, uploading, and wearing.

Amber had naturally dark hair and pale skin. She wasn't the thinnest girl, but she didn't think she was fat. However, judging by how these girls looked . . . maybe she was. Amber knew she'd have to change a whole lot if she wanted to fit in with them.

First, she convinced her mom to let her dye her hair. She told her mom that all the other girls at school had started dyeing their hair in sixth grade and she was behind. Her mom finally agreed, and Amber had her hair dyed over Christmas break. Blonde.

The popular girls went to the tanning bed almost every other day, but Amber was smart enough to know her pale skin would never tan, only burn to a crisp. So she did some research and found that one of the girls posted about a skin-care product that was a self-tanner. Amber bought it at the drugstore the next day after school.

Amber could tell right away her new efforts were working. When she showed up at school for the first time after Christmas break with her blonde hair and tan skin, people took notice.

She was the talk of the school that day.

Some people thought she was a new girl; others were just confused. Some people said she looked thinner; others said she looked fatter. Either way, the school was buzzing.

Amber walked into the bathroom after lunch, and there at the mirror, applying her lipstick, was Chloe. Amber tried to keep calm and collected, but a flurry of questions flooded her mind. *Will she notice me? Will she ignore me? Will she yell at me? Will she say I'm pretty?*

Amber walked to the sink and began applying a thick line of eyeliner. She could tell Chloe was watching but tried to play it cool.

Next thing she knew, Tiffany, Chloe's best friend, walked into the bathroom.

"Hey Chloe," she said, strutting in. "The boys want to show us Stephen's parents' lake house. His parents are out of town today and tomorrow!"

"Perfect." Chloe smiled. "We're ditching the rest of the day." She took one last look in the mirror. "All right, let's go."

She turned to Tiffany and began walking. As Tiffany walked beside Chloe, she motioned to Amber and asked, "Who's that?"

Chloe took a quick glance back and replied, "Don't know. But who cares?"

Tiffany quietly laughed and they walked out.

Amber was mortified. She had the hair and skin, but that wasn't enough. She knew she wasn't as skinny as they were. She burst into tears and decided one thing: she had to lose weight. And fast.

When she got home that night, she researched page after page about how to shed pounds. Most of the websites said weight would come off in a few months, but Amber didn't have that kind of time.

So she kept on searching until she found a possible solution: throwing up. Amber had heard girls at school talk about eating and then throwing up the food. She had even seen posts about it online.

The first time Amber tried it was horrible. She felt like her throat was choking. Her insides hurt. She felt lightheaded and thought she might faint. She was disgusted with herself and knew her parents would be so disappointed if they found out.

And she already thought God was disappointed in her. But it had to be done if she was ever going to be one of those girls.

A month later, Amber had lost ten pounds. She'd also convinced her dad to buy her some new clothes and had high hopes of where all this was headed. She walked around school with a strut and talked in more of a whisper like she had heard the other girls do. More and more people were taking notice of her.

It was working.

Something crazy happened one Friday morning. Amber stepped out of biology just as Chloe and Tiffany were taking a selfie. She knew this was her moment.

She walked up to the pair and asked, "Want me to take your picture?"

Chloe looked up. "Yes, thanks, girl!"

She handed Amber her phone as she and Tiffany posed together. Amber pushed the button and the picture snapped.

"Okay, now one of me and you." Chloe pointed at Amber.

"Huh?" Tiffany blurted out.

"No, really," Chloe said, giving Tiffany a look. "Here, come here . . . what's your name again?"

"Amber," she replied.

Chloe reached out and pulled Amber close for a picture. Amber smiled the biggest smile ever. Her moment was finally happening. Everything was about to change.

Amber was on cloud nine. She couldn't hear a thing her teachers were saying in her next two classes. All she could hear was Chloe's voice saying, "Okay, now one of me and you." She had finally made it! Everything had been worth it.

The bell rang. She was just about to get up from her seat when the kid in front of her busted out laughing. He passed his phone to the girl next to him. She tried to contain her hysteria. She quickly glanced over her shoulder at Amber and then looked away, laughing.

"What's going on?" Amber asked.

"Check Instagram."

Amber dug in her purse for her phone, clicked the Instagram icon, and saw what the girl was talking about. Chloe had tagged Amber in the picture of the two of them. Her post read, "My new BFF? #LOL #no #wannabe."

Amber couldn't believe it. This was the meanest thing anyone had ever done to her. The comments below the picture were even worse. The whole school was laughing and making fun of her.

She left school at lunch that day, so when she got home her parents were still at work. She used the key under the mat to get into the house. She walked into the kitchen and saw a kitchen knife.

She was stupid, ugly, fat, and no one liked her. People actually hated her. And now she hated everything about herself.

She picked up the knife. Her hands were shaking. She didn't know what to do.

Then, out of nowhere, she remembered a tweet about a new song that just released from a recording artist she followed online. Amber hadn't listened to it yet and decided that doing so would be her final act in life.

Amber started playing the song, and the chorus lyrics almost hit her in the face:

> My child, I understand what's really happening on
>   the inside
> I see the pain that you try to hide
> I know what's in your heart
> And I can see you for who you really are
> I'll fix what's broken on the inside

Amber began sobbing. She dropped the knife and her body began to tremble. She cried out to God, thanking Him for reminding her that He loved her. God was right there. He could help her. She felt like God's truth was washing over her, reminding her that she was enough.

Enough to just be herself.

I initially learned about Amber's story when she sent me a letter saying how my song "On the Inside" had impacted her. I was blown away by what I read in her letter. I still get choked up thinking about how God used the stillness of a song to help save Amber's life and move her back to Him.

Girls, learn from Amber's story. You are enough in God's eyes. You are loved. You are beautiful. You are treasured.

Quiet the noise of the world, the noise at your school, and listen to God's voice.

From Us Both

Life is so busy and crazy. Your thoughts are running a million miles an hour, even now. Allow yourself moments to slow down, quiet the noise, and spend time with God.

Your friends and your social media world will all have an opinion on what you should wear and who you should be. But maybe it's time to put down your phone, turn off your computer, and actually start living! Remember, the only voice that truly matters is God's.

Life is more beautiful when we take time to breathe and talk to Him.

3

The List

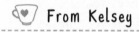 **From Kelsey**

Growing up, I made "The List."

You know the list I'm talking about. The one you've all made about your dream guy. I mean, let's face it. We all have that perfect guy in our minds. This guy has a list of qualities that make him the most amazing and wonderful guy ever. He will be our Prince Charming. We can totally picture him.

It's a beautiful thing to think this way.

It's okay to dream and pray for your future husband. I found that writing down these qualities helped me pray for him, even when he was just some imaginary guy on paper. I've always been a hopeless romantic, and I'm not ashamed of it.

—————xo—————

People say, "You know when you know." I never understood what that meant until Kyle. But I have to tell you, sometimes during my lonely years it felt like my list was so unrealistic. It felt like there could never be a guy out there who would really *truly* understand my heart.

If that's you, trust me, I completely understand.

I remember sitting in math class my sophomore year of high school when my friend leaned over and asked me what I was doing. To be honest with you, I wasn't paying attention to my teacher at all.

I was dreaming.

You see, it was one of those weeks where I just felt so alone. It seemed like all my friends had boyfriends except me. My heart longed to know what my life would look like outside of high school, and I was so over the boys at my school.

When my friend asked what I was doing, I explained to her that I was writing down a list. A list of characteristics and qualities that I wanted my future husband to have. I think she thought I was a little crazy, and I remember feeling kind of weird and embarrassed after telling her what I'd been doing. After all, she caught me writing a list and dreaming about this perfect imaginary guy in the middle of math class. But I truly didn't care. My parents raised me to believe in myself and to hold high standards.

All of a sudden my friend grabbed the piece of paper and started reading it to herself. She then started to quietly laugh. I was shocked and a little hurt that she would laugh at my list.

She whispered, "Wow, that's sort of an unrealistic list, don't ya think?" I felt about three feet small. I grabbed the piece of paper and slipped it into my backpack.

As I drove away from school that day, her words stayed with me. I got home, went upstairs to my parents' bedroom, and found my mom. I told her all about my day and about what my friend had said. I was feeling down.

Maybe it was true what she had said. *Was my list way too long? Was it unrealistic?* I remember sitting on my mom's bedroom floor for an hour just staring at the list I'd written. I also remember praying. Praying that God would show me if my list was too crazy.

My mom told me that of course my list wasn't unrealistic, that my dream guy—the one on paper—really was out there. After praying and talking with my mom, I felt a sense of hope for the future. And my friend was sort of right.

In the world's eyes my list *was* unrealistic. But God loves to do more than we could ever ask for or imagine if we chase after Him.

So my list was actually just perfect.

I tell you that story because there are moments (I had many of them) where it feels like the right guy is forever away. Or maybe you've made a list, but at times you've felt that your list is too much to ask for.

Well, I want you to be encouraged in the truth. The truth is, God loves when we dream about our future. God wants us to have high standards when it comes to boys and dating.

> God wants us to have high standards when it comes to boys and dating.

Never think that your list is too long or that your standards are too high. Keep adding to that list. And never ever

God loves to do *more* than we could *ever ask* for or *imagine* if we chase after Him.

for one second think, *My list is unrealistic*, or, *This guy that I've created on paper isn't out there.*

God knows, and His timing is perfect.

Dreaming about your future guy is not wrong. It's fun to think about what he will look like, or how he will dress, or what his personality will be like. You are a beautiful child of God, and His plans for you are outrageously exciting.

Remember, it's okay to have high standards. You should. So when you are bored in math class—make your list, pray for your future husband, and ultimately trust Jesus with it all. Even if the girl sitting next to you laughs.

God has such amazing plans for you, and you can trust Him with your happily ever after. So it's okay to dream and make a list. The trick is to make sure your list is filled with qualities worth waiting for. Qualities that have to do with his character. And then don't compromise on what you're looking for.

I've never been the type of girl to like the "bad boys," except for one stupid and embarrassing time. His name was Justin. We had known each other for years, but only as friends.

I would watch one girl after another get her heart broken because she thought Justin was actually going to change his bad-boy ways for her. Obviously, I knew I was never going to like Justin. I was clearly smarter than those girls who thought he was going to suddenly become nice.

Famous last words.

School was winding down and I could practically feel Christmas break approaching. Christmas is my favorite time of the year. As soon as Thanksgiving ended, my family turned on the Christmas music and started spreading cheer.

I've always enjoyed school, but we all know being home with your family, and especially home for *Christmas*, is way better than school. I couldn't wait to be on break. I had two final English essays to write and one history presentation to give.

A month earlier my history teacher assigned us partners for our final presentations. Any guesses on who my partner was? Yep. Justin.

Justin was extremely cute, and that meant every single girl wanted to date him or be his partner for a school project. But I just kept on reminding myself he was a bad boy. Justin was extremely flirty and charming when it came to girls, but he had absolutely no respect for teachers and parents. That wasn't his forte.

My parents had noticed that whenever my friends came by the house, Justin never stayed longer than ten minutes. He also never looked my dad in the eyes. And he was always wanting to spend time with me outside of my home, away from my family and parents.

I'm proud to tell you that I love my parents and we had a great relationship as I was growing up. But Justin was making me feel dumb for liking to hang out at home and for being friends with my parents. I had never had those feelings before.

Justin and I met a couple times outside of school to start talking about our presentation. Because I had known him for years, I knew his tricks and could sense that he was already trying to charm me.

"Well, would you look at us. Finally, after being friends for years, here we are . . . out on a date. You're a pretty lucky girl to be seen with me outside of school." Justin winked at me playfully. He had so much swag and arrogance that sometimes I thought his head was going to explode.

I laughed out loud. "Looks like you're the lucky one to be out with me. I know you've wanted this for years," I joked.

Justin's next sentence broke my heart. "Seriously, Kels, why do you think you are so much better than the rest of our friends? You never go to any of the parties. You really do act like you're better than me and everyone. We all think so."

Of course I got super defensive and started explaining how Justin's comment was completely unfair and not true at all. Justin rolled his eyes, then grabbed my hand. "Whatever. I just think because you go to church you think you're perfect . . . and you want a perfect guy."

I drove home and replayed our conversation over and over in my head about a hundred times. Everyone at school thought of me like that? My friends all thought I acted like I was better than them?

Have you ever felt like you are being misunderstood because you have high standards when it comes to guys or because you love God? That's exactly how I felt that night.

Justin sent me a text that night saying, "Kels, don't be sad about earlier. Would it help if I picked you up? I know a way to make you feel better . . ."

With any other guy I'd be like, "Sure, that sounds fun." But it was 11:00 on a school night and the text was from Justin. He had a reputation for being all sweet to girls and then turning right around and using them. Justin had hooked up with too many girls to count. Most of them were my friends.

Even though a little part of me wanted to go be with him that night, I had to say no. My parents are both very observant, and they could tell I was wrestling with the fact that I shouldn't like Justin but was already kind of crushing on him.

The day of our presentation things went great. We actually nailed it. And Justin didn't talk back to our teacher (I had begged him to show some respect while we were in front of the class). With the presentation behind us, Christmas finally arrived. And I couldn't be more excited to get away from school and from Justin. I knew he was bad for me, and the break would be nice.

The first night of break, while I was sitting by the fire drinking hot chocolate, my thoughts raced. I mean, my friends were all talking bad about me. Everyone thought I acted like I was better than them. I wasn't getting attention from any guys besides Justin, and that didn't even count. Justin was never going to be my boyfriend. During the time we had been partners for our school presentation Justin had hooked up with two other girls while flirting with me. Still, I wanted to see him all the time, and I was even hoping something would happen between the two of us.

So I grabbed my phone and texted Justin: "Wanna hang out? I'm free now if you are." Just typing the words was painful for me. I knew with everything inside of me that I shouldn't be texting him. He would only offer heartbreak. But that night I was so lonely I didn't care.

A brief thought flashed in my mind. I remembered my journal upstairs. The journal where I had made a list of what my dream guy would be like. The list where I had prayed about the traits I wanted in my future guy, and the journal where I had asked God to protect him from temptation. I quickly stifled the thought. Maybe my standards were too high?

Just asking the question broke my heart.

Justin didn't come inside. He just sent me a text saying he was outside waiting. I knew my parents didn't like when he did that, but that's how Justin rolled. I told my parents I would just be outside talking.

My mom pulled me aside and thoughtfully looked into my eyes. "Honey, please be careful with him. You are a one-in-a-million girl. God has great plans for you, and He has the most perfect guy already picked out for you. I don't think that guy is Justin. Anyway, I will have my phone with me if you need anything. I love you very much. Oh, and remember your list." She gave me a sweet look and smiled.

That night I did something that I still regret to this day. I kissed Justin in the driveway. I was so lonely. My list and my Prince Charming both felt like they were never going to happen for me. Justin was such a charmer, and he knew exactly what to say to get me to kiss him.

I didn't see Justin the rest of Christmas break, and I was devastated. Not because I thought he was going to magically turn into a good, faithful boyfriend, but because I had doubted God and His plans for my life. And I'd made a stupid mistake as a result of that doubt.

There is a reason the Bible says God's ways are far better than ours. His path is the one we should take. And His plans will lead us to joy and will spare our hearts from getting broken.

I used that situation with Justin as a reminder to never let go of my list, to never lose hope for my future husband, and to follow God and listen to His voice.

From that moment on I held to my high standards. And guess what? I'm so thankful I did. Being married to Kyle is the most amazing thing, and he surpasses everything that was on my list.

He really is my Prince Charming.

From Kyle

I had a list too, but there were no girls who fit the description when I was in high school. Actually, I never had a girlfriend in high school. I played sports, did musical theater, and was actively involved with other activities, but no girlfriend. I wanted one, but there weren't many Christian girls at my public high school to choose from.

The fall of my junior year a new girl showed up at our high school. Natalie. She was beautiful, charming, and came with a wild reputation. By the end of the week, everybody at our school knew just how wild she was.

Natalie took a special interest in me. She flirted with me every chance she got, and she surprised me by asking me to go with her to the winter formal dance. Normally the guys ask the girls.

Even though it was forward of her to ask me, I was tired of being single. So I said yes and made plans to take Natalie to the dance. It was exciting. I was attracted to her.

Still, I didn't want to compromise my faith. Part of me thought that this date could provide an opportunity for me to talk to her about the deeper side of life. Maybe even share what I believed.

But the truth is, that was just part of me.

On the night of the winter formal, I showed up at Natalie's house expecting to meet her parents before the dance, but they weren't home. Natalie had failed to mention that they were out of town.

Natalie and her friends were dancing around the kitchen. She asked if I wanted something to help loosen me up. I said no and reminded Natalie that she'd told me there wouldn't be any alcohol tonight. With a flirty laugh, Natalie reassured me there would not be.

As we made our way outside to my car, Natalie told me it would be fun for us to ride in her friend's larger car so the group could all be together. I hesitated but then went along. We got in her friend's car and drove off. Music pounded out the windows.

When we were about a block from the school, the car stopped. Natalie's friend turned around and asked if everyone wanted to go around the block one more time. Some of the girls started to giggle.

They screamed, "Yes!" from the backseat. I could sense things were about to get crazy, so I said, "Let's just go to the dance. We're already here." Natalie's friend put her foot on the gas pedal and began to drive.

"Stop!" I yelled. "Just let me out here!"

The car slowed and I opened the door and got out. Through the window Natalie said, "We'll be just a little while. See you soon!"

The car sped off. I walked to the school and waited for Natalie and her friends to arrive. Thirty minutes later they finally pulled into the parking lot. Natalie got out of the car and ran into my arms with a huge smile on her face.

Her breath reeked of alcohol.

Once inside, Natalie and her friends started dancing crazily to the music. I was so embarrassed. I couldn't believe my date was completely drunk. She began to grab and pull at me to grind with her, but I just kept my distance a few feet away while smiling and pretending to dance.

I didn't want her to get upset and start going really crazy while she was drunk. It was all so awkward. After a few songs Natalie told me, "Me and the girls are going to the restroom. Be right back."

I waited by the wall of the gym for Natalie to return but was actually thankful she had left. I finally had a moment of peace. Until I realized I didn't have any way home. My car was at Natalie's house. Her friends, who were now all drunk, had driven us here.

This was turning into the worst night of my life.

I watched the door for another twenty minutes, but Natalie never came back. I finally walked toward the bathroom to make sure she was okay, but lights through a window caught my eye. Flashing blue and white lights.

The police.

I headed to the nearest exit and opened the door. There in front of me was Natalie, pressed against a cop car in handcuffs. She mouthed "so sorry" and then began to laugh hysterically. She looked insane. The cop opened the door to the backseat of the police car and pushed Natalie inside.

Could the night get any worse? I figured it might when I had to call my parents to explain the situation and ask them to pick me up.

Much to my surprise, my parents were actually pretty awesome about it. They picked me up and we had a good talk about the kind of girls I was giving my heart to. A talk that reminded me this entire crazy situation could have been avoided if I had just stuck to my convictions about who I should and shouldn't date.

-----χ0----~

When I first met Kelsey, I thought, "Okay, this girl's cute!" But I wouldn't have pursued her unless I saw that she had a heart for God, that she loved Jesus, and that it naturally showed by how she lived her life.

I saw from the first moment I met her that Kelsey had confidence. Not in an arrogant way or because she knew she was beautiful. Rather, it was a quiet confidence that I am convinced is from God.

Kelsey was confident in her identity as a child of God and confident in front of guys. She wasn't shy *or* flirty. She wasn't trying to be the loudest person in the room. She was just Kelsey. She was confident in her singleness and confident that God would bring the right man into her life.

She didn't tell me any of these things the first time I met her. (It would have been weird if she did!) But it didn't take long for me to figure all these things out. She loved people and she loved God, and it showed.

Kelsey also dressed classy. Natalie had dressed, well . . . pretty skanky. Their outfits couldn't have been more different. But guess which one looked sexier? Kelsey, hands down!

Dressing classy doesn't mean you dress boring. It just means you don't have to give it all away like Natalie did. Choosing to dress classy allows there to be more of a mystery, and ladies, guys love some mystery.

Dressing slutty will get you the quick attention, but not the kind of attention you really want or from the guys you want the attention from. Trust me, I'm a guy. I know. You'd be horrified to hear the kinds of things some guys say about girls who dress slutty. They talk about the girls as if they are sexual objects instead of actual people with souls and feelings. It's sad and awful.

Most guys don't value girls who show lots of skin. So while Natalie came across as desperate, Kelsey came across as confident. Confidence is so much sexier.

-----XO-----

We all have a list. Whether you've written it down in your journal or stored it away in your mind, you have an idea of the person you want to date or marry. But right this minute I want to challenge you to prioritize your list. If I had done that, I would never have ended up in that mess with Natalie. I would have been more cautious, and I would have realized that just because I thought a girl was pretty, that didn't make her *the* girl.

The right guy is looking for more than just good looks, and you should be too.

Just like girls make lists, guys do the same thing. Wouldn't you want to know exactly what a godly guy wants? Well, I can point you in the right direction, to the book of Proverbs in the Bible—the wisest book on the planet. Take a look at what it says about beauty and character.

> Charm is deceptive, and beauty does not last;
> but a woman who fears the LORD will be
> greatly praised.
>
> Proverbs 31:30 NLT

The word "fear" in this verse means to respect and have a deep reverence for God. Girls, the right guy will place significance on your character, confidence, and passion for Jesus. The perfect combination is when you find someone who gets your heart racing but also has a deep and genuine faith. What a beautiful combination. It doesn't have to be one or the other.

Attractive *or* Christian? He can be both! If you don't know that guy, then be patient. You just haven't met him yet.

A handsome guy who doesn't love God will lead you down the

> *The right guy is looking for more than just good looks.*

wrong path and break your heart. A Christian guy you're not attracted to obviously won't work either. I encourage you to pray for the guy of your dreams the way I prayed for my dream girl, Kelsey.

I believed there was a beautiful girl who loved Jesus with as much passion as I did. I prayed for her. I believed she was real.

You need to do the same with the guy on your list. God says to pray believing.

Whatever you've placed on your list regarding your special guy, add one more thing: a commitment to purity. This was another item I had on my list for my future wife. The right guy will be looking for someone pure. It will be on his list too. Remember that.

A quick note: Some people don't learn about the beauty and importance of purity until it's too late. If that's you or someone you love, remember this—Jesus asks us to come to Him and repent, which means turning away from our sin and turning to Him. You can choose purity today. A fresh start. A new beginning. It's never too late with Jesus.

-----XO-----

Finally, whenever you think about the person God has for you . . . pray. Pray that God will protect him and his family. Pray for his purity. Pray for his relationship with Jesus. As you're praying for your future guy, also pray that God will guide you to be the right girl for him.

God says to pray believing.

That way when you meet him, you'll be amazed at how he is "the list." And he'll be amazed by the same thing in you. Neither of you will be perfect people, but you'll both be chasing after God. God's plans for your life are that beautiful.

From Us Both

You are a one-in-a-million girl. God has a plan and a purpose for your life. Never lose sight of how special you are. Make a list of characteristics and qualities you would love to see in your future dream guy. Keep having high standards when it comes to guys and dating.

Trust us, you won't regret it!

4

Call Me Maybe

☕ From Kelsey

When you think of your ideal guy, what do you envision? A gentleman, perhaps? A strong Christian? Someone who is hilariously funny? A deep and passionate sort of a person? Kind? Respectful?

Sometimes it's hard to believe there are actually good guys out there. Unfortunately, a lot of guys we know can be the wrong ones. Now, this isn't a chapter bashing guys. But it is a real look at some major turnoffs and red flags to be aware of.

Remember, it's okay to have high standards!

This may sound cheesy to some of you, or it may sound accurate, but I honestly believe the biggest turnoff in a guy is when he doesn't put God first. I say that in the most loving, nonjudgmental way possible.

When a guy follows Jesus and puts Him first, he will be the best leader he can be. Guys who don't put God first in their life will be the biggest heartbreak for us girls. Guys were created to lead. It's in their nature to lead. You want a guy to lead in a loving, godly way. When a guy is walking with the Lord and is reading his Bible, you will be able to tell.

-----XO-----

Let's talk a little bit more about this whole idea of guys being leaders. I've noticed that lots of girls have a really hard time letting guys actually lead.

Now, I want to be clear that I'm not trying to offend girls with this statement. I'm a girl, and I know how strong, powerful, educated, brave, funny, and enlightening we are. I believe those traits are very important to have. But I also know that it is completely biblical to let a guy lead, even if that's not always a popular opinion.

One small way to start? Give the guys in your life room to be gentlemen. In fact, insist on it!

The other day I was at a coffee shop and observed an interesting scene. I was at a corner table doing some work on my laptop (and of course sipping one of my favorite coffee drinks, an Americano). It's sort of hard not to people watch when I'm out and about, but especially in a coffee shop. So many people come and go.

Anyway, I was sitting there when all of a sudden I saw a woman waving her arms in the air, and let's just say her face did *not* look happy. The woman made such a scene that people at several other tables stopped and stared at what was going on.

A guy, a total stranger to the woman, had tried to hold the door open for her. He wanted to be polite and let her go inside before him, and that was all it took for the woman to completely lose her cool. She was rolling her eyes and waving her hands in a "get out of my life" kind of way.

I sat there in shock. The kind man quickly apologized and turned away with embarrassment and defeat in his eyes.

In a quick blur the woman ordered her latte and left the coffee shop. But I couldn't shake the image of the guy's face or the look in his eyes. He was only trying to be a gentleman, something our society would have praised him for not too long ago. This story may sound extreme or made up, but the sad reality is that it's not.

As girls, we need to remember that guys need to be built up, complimented, and respected. They also need to be able to open up doors for us.

But it goes even deeper than that. Jesus calls all of us to love one another. Let's start living that way. Let's be the kind of girls who build up others and give out compliments often. After all, compliments are free.

Girls, let's allow godly guys to lead us. Not in a dominating way but in a loving, biblical way. You will know if your boyfriend is putting God first in his life by the way he leads you. You will see it in his actions. When it comes to relationships, guys can do a lot of things wrong, but sometimes it's our fault for being with the wrong type of guy.

----xo----

I had a friend in college who had been dating the same guy for two years. Things seemed to be getting more serious for the two of them. The way that their relationship worked was he sort of ran the show. Now, I'm all for a guy leading, but not in a selfish, mean, ungodly way. And those were the ways this guy was basically leading my friend.

I can remember getting ready for our Wednesday night chapel service on campus and texting my friend to ask if she and her boyfriend would be at chapel. Her response was always the same. She would say that her boyfriend didn't want her to go because he thought other guys would talk to her and flirt with her at chapel. Yikes!

Obviously you and I can see red flags all over this situation, but my friend couldn't. Sadly, she was "in love" with him. Her heart wasn't willing to let her see him for who he truly was.

One day she came to me sobbing because her boyfriend was threatening to break up with her. I was thinking this could be the start of an amazing new chapter for my sweet friend. She of course was devastated.

I asked her why he was threatening to break up, and she said, "He saw me talking to another guy after class and he is convinced that I'm cheating on him." I couldn't believe the madness I was hearing. You see, I had a class with her boyfriend, and I really couldn't stand the guy. He was the biggest flirt ever. He even flirted with me!

I had tried explaining this to my friend at one point, and she had snapped at me. But here she was with tears streaming down her face because her boyfriend had the nerve to think she was cheating on him.

I've noticed that usually the guys who are crazy jealous of you are the very same guys flirting and charming every other girl. Totally not okay. They don't trust you because they know exactly what they are doing when you're not around:

flirting with other people. So they think maybe you're doing the same thing they are.

I tried to be there for my friend. She and her boyfriend had many ups and downs that year. I would look at their situation and feel thankful that I wasn't stuck in that kind of relationship.

The sad reality of my friend's situation will always stay with me. After watching that relationship play out, I knew two things. One, her boyfriend was not putting God first. He was mean, controlling, and took advantage of her and her kindness, all while flirting with other girls. And two, I wanted to be with a guy who did put God first no matter what. A guy who puts God first will in return treat me like I should be treated.

> *It's far better to be single than to be with the wrong guy.*

Why is it that we would rather compromise our morals, our personalities, and sometimes even our beliefs just to have a boyfriend? No guy should have that much power over your heart. A guy who comes into your life and then negatively changes everything about you . . . well, that guy is not worth falling for.

Trust me, it's far better to be single than to be with the wrong guy.

----xo----

During my junior year of high school I had a real life "call me maybe" moment. I decided to be homeschooled that year because, to be honest, I was pretty sick of my high school.

My school was very cliquish, and it seemed like gossip was a required class.

I cared deeply for my friends, but I continued to feel misunderstood. I didn't go to the parties, and by then the invitations had stopped. I was really trying to follow God and chase after Him.

All of that to say, being homeschooled was the biggest blessing. A break from all of the drama. I was able to wake up and do school in my pajamas—I mean, how amazing is that? I would usually finish all of my work one to two hours before my friends got out of school. It was wonderful. I also was able to focus more on acting, singing, and dancing.

I was in a dance class with some of my friends and one new guy who none of us had seen before. He was buff and tan. Quite the mystery to us girls.

One day after class he and I got to talking. In our short conversation he mentioned many of his accomplishments, even using the words, "I'm kind of a big deal." I knew right then and there that no matter how handsome this guy was, he wasn't someone I wanted to date. We would have to just be friends.

I mean, come on! Who actually says that to someone?

Somehow the guy managed to save the conversation and had us both laughing before I turned and walked out to my car. The next week he apologized for talking so much about himself: "I'm sorry for last week. I only just met you, and you don't need to be bothered with my schedule or the fact that I will be filming a movie this weekend."

I was just smiling up at him when he leaned a little closer and said, "So, I'll be done shooting my scenes around 7:00 on Saturday night. Call me maybe?"

I couldn't believe it. It took everything inside of me not to laugh out loud. Gosh, he was so cute, but he was going about it completely the wrong way. I'm all for someone being confident, but this guy was downright arrogant. Needless to say, I didn't call him.

Have you ever had a guy be that cocky and arrogant toward you? Some guys operate under the false pretense that girls should run after them. They think that when they act all "swag" we should just fall at their feet.

Girls, you shouldn't have to chase a guy. He should be chasing and pursuing you. And don't settle for a guy who will only talk about himself and never ask how you are doing. That's not cool.

Our culture tells us girls to go after the guy and call him first. So many messages are thrown at us to be forward. That's completely backwards. I know it's hard, but try and let the guy make the first move.

Let the guy text or call you first. Of course there are exceptions, and this isn't some magic rule. But dare to be different. Stand out from the crowd. And if your phone isn't blowing up . . . be patient, pray, and wait.

Before you consider dating someone, look at how he treats others. Is he kind? Humble? Does he care about other people?

> Don't date a guy just to have a boyfriend. You're worth more than that.

And remember . . . never ever date someone who doesn't put God first. It's the biggest turnoff there is and will only leave your heart shattered.

One of the things that really drew me to Kyle was that I could tell he was chasing after God, and it was so attractive. But here's the tricky thing: even when you meet the most amazing guy and he is putting God first, resist the urge to make the first move. Let the guy chase you.

Never ever settle, girls. You are deeply loved by God. You are beautiful and extremely valuable in His eyes. Don't date a guy just to have a boyfriend. You're worth more than that.

From Kyle

Olivia was a sweet girl I knew back in Pennsylvania, a girl who dreamed about marriage. She longed for that day when she could say "I do." The dream consumed her. Because of this, her relationships with guys were fast and furious.

One summer, my longtime high school friend Jake ran into Olivia at the gym. Olivia called me and told me how they met. I was on my way to dinner with Kelsey, but Olivia never gave me the chance to explain that I was busy. She was desperate for information.

"Hey." She sounded beyond giddy. "So . . . I met your friend Jake. He's amazing!"

"Jake?" Before I could say another word, she cut me off.

"What can you tell me about him? I mean, where's he from originally?"

My mind raced. "New York, I think."

"Really? Perfect. And he has a sister, right? About my age?" Olivia had a thousand questions.

"His sister?" *Where was this going?*

"Yeah, Jake told me about her. I found her on Twitter. She seems super sweet, so yeah, I'm going to reach out to her. Right? Isn't that a great idea?"

I could barely keep up with Olivia's random questions. "Okay . . ."

"And what's his favorite color? I want to buy him a cute card for next time we hang out."

She rattled off a few more questions and the conversation was over before I had time to process what was happening. I set down my phone and Kelsey looked at me. "Babe, what in the world was that?" She laughed—probably because of the confused look on my face.

"Ha-ha! Yeah, I think Olivia likes Jake." I shook my head, baffled. "Two of my friends from Philly. Crazy."

"Ya think?" Kelsey smiled.

I chuckled again. "She had a *lot* of questions."

Olivia wanted to know everything she could about Jake. His work, his family, his faith, his favorite colors. She had something planned, that was for sure.

A few days later, I began noticing something on social media. Olivia had become close friends with Jake's sister, Miranda. Extremely close. At least it looked that way on Twitter. If the pictures were proof, the two girls were hanging out with each other almost every day.

Olivia somehow managed to connect with her all because of her new interest in Jake. I never found out exactly how Olivia "bumped into" Jake's sister. Regardless, they suddenly were together every day.

They began posting online as "best friends forever." It all seemed pretty sudden. I mean, they had just met. Olivia grew closer and closer to Jake's sister, which allowed her more time to hang around Jake.

I was grabbing lunch one day when Jake called me.

"Hey, how's it going?"

"Things are good . . . I guess." He sounded confused. "It's just Olivia. It's like this whirlwind thing, and I kind of don't really know what's happening."

I found a place to sit down. "Didn't you two just meet?"

"Yeah." He hesitated. "Anyway, she's been sending me these crazy love memes all day. I think she's trying to be funny."

I couldn't help but laugh. "Let's hope so! You guys texting a lot?"

"Yeah, well, she's been hanging with my sister, so I see her all the time because of that. She started texting me earlier this week. We'll have to see what happens."

A few weeks later he called again. Apparently some friends came over to his house for a movie night—and Olivia invited herself to join them. During the film, Jake told me, Olivia reached down and grabbed his hand. But she didn't just hold his hand, she began to caress it with both of hers. Jake said he was very confused.

"I mean, I'm not even sure if we're actually dating," he told me.

He said at the end of the movie, right before the credits started rolling, Olivia stood up, took Jake's hand, and led him to the door. Then she turned to his friends—gathered at *his* house—and said, "Sorry we can't stay. We can't be late for dessert at my parents' house. Have a great night, guys!"

"What did you do?" I plopped down on my sofa. Olivia's behavior shocked me.

"I didn't feel like I had a choice." Jake still sounded bewildered. "I went with her."

We ended that phone call with Jake asking me a question. "So am I a happy guy on an adventurous new romance . . . or is this all something Olivia's making up?"

Jake made a good point. I didn't know either.

A week later I was on the phone with Jake and asked, "Hey man, how you doing?"

"I'm good . . . I think," he said, almost trying to convince himself. "You wouldn't believe the strange week I had."

"Try me."

"Well, it's still about Olivia." He sighed. I couldn't quite tell if he was smiling.

"Yeah, what's going on with you guys?"

With a slight laugh he replied, "Yeah, that's over."

"Oh . . . okay. Well, it sounds like you're not too bummed out."

"Dude, the whole thing was such a trip. I mean, at first she totally caught my eye," he gushed. "But her forwardness quickly became annoying and desperate."

"Yikes. I get that."

"It felt like I was performing a part in a play." Jake let out a breath of frustration. "First, we meet, then she's best friends with my sister. Next thing I know, we're kind of dating . . . I think? At least it looks that way all over her Instagram. And then we're at her parents' house talking about how we should plan Thanksgiving together."

"Whoa . . . what? You serious?"

Jake was serious.

The poor guy never had the chance to lead the relationship. Olivia got his number that first day they met at the gym.

Stalked him online. Grabbed his hand. Invited him over . . . and on and on. He couldn't act like a man with her.

She led their "relationship." It was all too much, too fast. She didn't wait for him to pursue her, and in the end, all her efforts became unattractive to Jake.

Olivia wanted a guy . . . a relationship . . . a marriage *now*. She didn't wait for the guy to pursue her. She took matters into her own hands and manipulated situations in order to make Jake be with her.

Ladies, don't do this!

Later, Olivia called me and told me how embarrassed she was at her actions.

Guys are made to be leaders. We want to do the pursuing. Don't make things so easy for us. If you like a guy but he isn't doing anything about it, resist forcing the relationship. You can manipulate yourself into a situation, but it won't work.

Have patience. Trust God's timing. Don't rush it. Let him pursue you. Feel free to give subtle signs that you are into him (we find these very helpful, in fact), but don't lead the relationship for him.

If you like a guy but he isn't doing anything about it, resist forcing the relationship.

If a godly guy you're interested in isn't making the move, then maybe he's not the one for you. Or maybe he is not ready for a relationship. Again, have patience. It's better to be single and wait for the right guy than to be with the wrong guy when the right guy shows up.

----xO----

Another friend of mine, Peter, was the victim of a girl who had to have the attention of multiple guys. Her name was Jill. Nice Christian girl, super fun. Again, the girls in this chapter aren't bad girls. They are just chasing the wrong things.

Jill loved attention. Peter was just one of the many boys she hung out with and texted with and flirted with. She always seemed to have more than one guy in her back pocket. She texted numerous guys at the same time with her signature flirty charm.

Peter had been Jill's friend for years. He was a consistent, good friend. Even when Jill was dating a guy named Sam, Peter wasn't jealous or bitter. He didn't ever try to cause problems between them or break them up. He was just a good friend.

One fall day, Sam broke up with Jill. She was devastated, and Peter was there to console her. He helped her heart heal, and in the process he developed feelings for her. He realized that those feelings were always kind of there, but now he could act on them because she was single.

Peter knew that Jill loved attention from multiple guys. He had seen it firsthand for years. But Peter began to feel that Jill was turning over a new leaf with guys, possibly changing for the better. He felt like she was directing her attention solely on him.

She told Peter that she had stopped texting Sam and that Sam wasn't good for her. She was ready to move on. Peter couldn't have been more thrilled. He wasn't about to ask her out or anything like that, but he could envision a future with them together.

Find your *identity* in *God*, not in *guys*.

One night Peter was driving home from school and decided to stop by the mall where Jill worked. He texted her, "Hey, I'm driving by the mall. I'm gonna stop in your store."

Jill quickly replied, "Oh . . . Peter, I'm at home sick. Not feeling very well."

Peter texted back, "Okay. I'll pray for you to feel better."

As he passed the mall he decided to go in and grab some Chick-fil-A from the food court before heading home. He walked through the mall, and as he rounded the corner to the food court, he saw Jill and Sam sitting down at a table holding hands.

Jill looked up and was horrified to see Peter. Peter was stunned. Jill stood up and began to whimper, "Peter, I'm sorry," but Peter turned and quickly walked away.

Peter was heartbroken. He felt betrayed and lost all confidence in Jill ever changing. Their future had been ruined by Jill's dishonesty and her inability to stop reaching out to numerous guys for attention. Their friendship was damaged for a long time and nothing romantic ever happened between them.

> A wise woman builds her home,
>   but a foolish woman tears it down with her
>   own hands.
>
> Proverbs 14:1 NLT

Ladies, don't be a player. Be wise. Don't be the girl who is always flirting. Be wise. Being a player and being a flirt will tear down your relationships.

Trust me, I know guys are guilty of this too. Looking back, I was way too flirty growing up. I broke quite a few hearts by accident . . . and some not by accident. But I'm responsible for that. I don't take that lightly.

Your words and attention go far with guys. Have respect for guys and have respect for yourself. Don't be so available. Find your identity in God, not in guys.

----xo----

When your identity is found in Christ, you won't have to be someone you're not. I've met tons of girls who feel like they have to dumb themselves down around guys. They are intelligent girls, but when guys come into the mix, they feel they have to resort to this airheaded version of themselves.

Let me just say, that's not cute. That's stupid. It's unattractive. It comes across as an act and doesn't allow for any depth to occur . . . or a real conversation to start. Acting like an airhead doesn't grab a guy's heart. Don't be forgettable. Be who God made you to be . . . unforgettable!

The guys you want to end up with—Christlike, kind, faithful, bold, considerate guys—are turned off by girls who are forward. Your forwardness might catch the attention of some guys, but they will be the wrong kind of guys—lazy, afraid, pushovers, followers.

Don't try to run your love life.

If you do, it will fail miserably. Trust God and pray for your future husband, believing he is out there. Pray for him to be a leader. Pray for him to make bold decisions for God and for you. Pray that you will be ready and mature in your faith when he shows up in your life.

When I first met Kelsey, she didn't try to catch my attention in a flirty way and she didn't have tons of guys she was texting. Kelsey was just awesome. She was fun, friendly, and humble. Her love for God was evident. She was comfortable in her own skin. Her beauty and confidence lit up the room.

That's what drew me to her. And when we began our relationship, she let me lead. She didn't manipulate or maneuver situations so we could be together. She let me make the moves. I finally found a girl who let me chase her.

And I get to keep on chasing her the rest of my life.

From Us Both

Should you call him? Should you not call him? The choice is yours. Just know that when you make the first move, it can come across as a little desperate. Guys like when a girl is more of a mystery so they have something to chase!

5

R-E-S-P-E-C-T

From Kelsey

Girls, you have more power than you think when it comes to guys.

That may sound a little funny, but it's true. We girls have the power to build up our guys or tear them down. We have a choice to show the guys in our life disrespect or respect. When we respect someone we show them love.

When I hear the word *love* I immediately think of the word *respect*. Love and respect go hand in hand. You certainly can't love someone if you don't respect them. And you don't respect someone you don't love.

Jesus showed us love by dying on the cross for our sins. He loved us then, and He continues to display love for us every single day. God loves you so much, and He will forever cherish your heart.

I want to be the kind of person who shows love and respect toward others, and most importantly toward my husband, Kyle. Every healthy and amazing relationship needs both love and respect to thrive. But first you need to have love and respect for yourself before you enter a relationship.

What you say with your words and how you act shows where your relationship is at and where it will be in the future.

> *You need to have love and respect for yourself before you enter a relationship.*

Girls, I want to encourage you to build up the guys in your life. We should be the kind of godly girls who display love and respect.

I love studying relationships, and growing up in a big family teaches you a lot about them. What I've discovered is that relationships thrive on love and respect. The perfect example of this is God.

God displays perfect love toward us. He isn't forceful with us; He respects us. And the amazing thing is, He is always there waiting for us to come to Him. God wants a relationship with *you*. After all, He is the one who created relationships.

---- XO ----

It was the beginning of autumn. The air was crisp. The leaves were crunchy and brilliantly scattered underneath my feet in vibrant oranges, yellows, and reds. As I walked to my very first college class that morning, I couldn't help but

look up to the sky, take a deep breath, and smile. I was super
excited and nervous for college.

I had no idea what the workload would be like. Would
my professors be intensely scary like in the movies, or would
they be wonderful? College was such a mystery, but I couldn't
wait to get started. With my coffee in hand, a new cute bag
filled with school supplies, and God going before me, I was
ready. English 101, here I come!

The professor greeted all of us students with a warm,
friendly smile. She passed out the syllabus and then told us
to say hi to the person next to us. I already liked her.

I got out my notebook and pen and said hi to the girl next
to me. Her name was Brittany. We discovered very quickly
that we had so much in common. Both of us loved to sing,
dance, and act. Like me, Brittany did musical theater while
growing up. Our small talk naturally turned to boys and
if we were dating anyone. I was single, but Brittany had a
boyfriend.

Our professor directed everyone's attention back up front
and the rest of class went wonderfully. By the end of that first
English class I knew three things: one, I loved my professor;
two, God had brought me a sweet new friend in Brittany;
and three, Brittany and her boyfriend weren't doing the best.

A week went by and I ran into Brittany and her boyfriend
at a coffee shop near campus. I ran up, gave her a hug, and
said hi to her boyfriend. It felt like I had just stepped into
a really awkward situation . . . maybe even a fight between
the two of them. So I took that as my cue to go order my
coffee.

While waiting for my drink, I overheard Brittany say, "You
are so dumb. I mean, how could you get that question wrong

on the test? Even my five-year-old brother would have gotten that one right!"

She didn't stop there. "Seriously, sometimes I think I'm dating a sixth-grade boy." She tried to offer a smile like she was just joking, but he wasn't looking up. He just stared at the floor, defeated and embarrassed.

I scrambled for my phone. You know how you try to look busy when you're actually listening to someone's conversation? Yeah, that was me. I could tell Brittany realized that all she had been doing for the last ten minutes was cutting her boyfriend down. She tried to cover it up by smiling occasionally. But based on his posture, I could tell the guy was hurting.

The barista finally called out my name and placed my order on the bar. I glanced over at Brittany's table and saw they were just sitting there in awkward silence. I gave her a quick wave and headed out to my car.

The whole drive back to campus I couldn't get that scene out of my mind. Brittany had completely disrespected her boyfriend by publicly tearing him down. My heart was hurting for him and for Brittany.

Brittany was a great friend to me. She was kind and sweet and a lot of fun, but how she treated her boyfriend would negatively affect their relationship forever.

Before I knew it the semester was almost over, and school had been such a delight. College didn't turn out to be scary like I had worried about. I actually loved it and was excited to learn more and more. Brittany had a tough semester, though.

Her boyfriend broke up with her.

His reasons for ending things with her were no surprise to me. He told her she made him feel like he couldn't do anything right. He also said that even though they had some amazing times, the times where she would tear him down or randomly freak out at him stood out the most.

Brittany couldn't see the hurt she was causing her boyfriend by bringing him down, tearing at his heart, not loving him the best, and ultimately not respecting him. And I learned something from her experience that will forever stay with me: guys *need* to be built up, and they *need* to be respected.

My mom taught me the importance of words. Words can build someone up or they can tear someone down. We all need to hear kind, loving, and respectful words. We call them "words of affirmation," which means using words to affirm and build someone else up. Have you been in a situation where someone has brought you down with their words?

Words matter so much.

It's easy to gossip with our friends or disrespect someone, but what if we all paused before we talked? What if every single word out of your mouth and out of my mouth was kind? What if we used our words to uplift others? Let's do that.

Let's make sure our words speak love, kindness, and respect to the people around us.

----xo----

I grew up in a house where guys were everywhere. Between my dad, five younger brothers, and their friends—yeah, I'd say my mom and I were outnumbered. But honestly, I loved it. I learned so much.

I had the privilege of watching my mom treat my dad with such love and respect. I watched my dad treat my mom like a queen and show her love and respect. It goes both ways.

Girls, not only do you need to respect the guys in your life, but they need to respect you. You are a prized jewel, and you deserve the utmost love and respect.

Compliments are an easy way to lift someone up, to show them you care about them and respect them. And guess what? Compliments are *free*. So why not try and give them out as much as possible? When someone gives you a compliment, how do you feel? You feel special and you feel noticed.

Play a little game with yourself. Try to give out as many real compliments as you possibly can in one day. Then give out even more compliments the next day. Before you know it, complimenting and thinking of others will become a beautiful habit.

When we take our eyes off our own lives and focus on others, we become the prettiest versions of ourselves. Giving someone else a compliment allows us to experience instant joy.

In the seasons when I was single, my mom would encourage me to give compliments to my brothers and to my dad. Then, when the time came and I had a boyfriend, or when I was ready to get married, I would be prepared to give as many genuine compliments as possible. I loved that advice and have followed it ever since.

----xo----

Sometimes love and respect look like sacrifice. People in our lives will let us down and our hearts will get hurt, but those situations are the true tests to see if we can still give out free compliments.

Are we willing to show love and respect to others even when it's hard, or when they don't deserve love and respect

When we take our eyes

off our own lives and

focus on others,

we become the

prettiest versions

of ourselves.

according to our standards? Are we willing to give words of affirmation to someone who is being mean to us?

These are questions I think about. And in the end, yes, we are still supposed to show respect to that friend or family member, which is really showing that person God's love.

When God brought Kyle into my life, it seemed obvious to me from the beginning that he was the one for me. When we were dating, I prayed all the time that God would show me very quickly if Kyle really was the guy for me. God revealed to me and to Kyle that we were meant to be together forever.

I respected him enough to let him lead the entire pace of our dating. Kyle completely pursued me. That's right, I made him work! He was the first one to tell me he liked me. He was the first one to ask if he could hold my hand. And he was the first one to ask if he could kiss me good night.

Sometimes I felt impatient and wanted to push things along. I was falling more in love with Kyle with every passing day, and I *so* wanted to tell him out loud. But I waited for him and followed his lead. And I'm glad I did.

When Kyle first told me, "Baby, I'm in love with you. I love you so much," my heart had never felt so alive. By not jumping the gun and acting on my own passionate feelings, I allowed Kyle the space and freedom to truly take the lead. All of those huge moments in our relationship were led by him.

Girls, when you let a guy lead you in a godly way, there's no better feeling. We need to remember that we can't show love unless we show respect and let the guy lead.

If you aren't dating, practice words of affirmation on the guys God has placed in your life right now. Your dad. Your brothers. Your guy friends. You will begin to notice a change in the way they carry themselves. And remember, don't be like my friend Brittany. Be careful with your words because they can do some real damage to a guy's heart.

Girls, we were made to love and build others up, and guys were made to lead us in sacrificial love. This is no accident. God planned it this way. By doing these things you will be showing your guy or the guys in your life that you love and respect them.

Love and respect applies to all of the relationships in your life: friends, family, parents, siblings, teachers, youth group leaders. Be the kind of girl who displays love and respect for all people. By loving people and respecting them, the relationships in your life will change for the better.

Give away compliments and focus on other people. It will help keep your heart beautiful on the inside, and you will be much happier on the outside.

The actress Audrey Hepburn said, "I believe that happy girls are the prettiest girls." Exactly! Thanks, Audrey. Now go be pretty and spread love to the world. Let the guy lead you in a godly way. Show respect. And give away as many compliments as you can.

From Kyle

Once upon a time, Robbie met Amanda.

Robbie had just finished his baseball season and was excited to enjoy the summer at home. He was single, and had been for a while. He told people he was waiting for the right girl.

Amanda had just gotten out of a two-year relationship and had a string of flings before the night she met Robbie.

The two met through mutual friends, and their conversation took off. Robbie never claimed to be hilariously funny, but by the way Amanda was laughing (loudly) at everything he said, anyone else would have thought he was a stand-up comedian. As the pair talked, they realized they shared a love for the outdoors. They both enjoyed hiking and bike rides.

After a few hours, Robbie's friends started heading out and called for him to join them. Before Robbie turned to his friends Amanda asked, "Hey, what's your number? We should hang out sometime." They exchanged numbers and Robbie left with a smile on his face.

The next morning Robbie woke up to a text from Amanda. "Hey! Loved meeting you last night. Some friends and I are going downtown for the music festival. Wanna come?"

Robbie was surprised by the text. He thought it was a little bold. But he was also anxious to have a girlfriend and thought maybe something could develop with Amanda. After all, she did think he was hilarious.

Robbie showed up to the concert later that night, and Amanda couldn't have been happier. They sang, danced, and laughed all night. As they walked back to the parking lot, Amanda reached for Robbie's hand and locked her fingers between his. She held on tight until they arrived at her car where she hugged Robbie and held the embrace for a solid ten seconds.

The next few days were a texting marathon. Amanda initiated every conversation. Robbie could barely keep up.

Later that week, Amanda called Robbie and invited him to her house for dinner. They talked about their favorite family memories, best ice cream flavors, past relationships

. . . even marriage. Amanda was the one who brought up marriage. She told Robbie how she couldn't wait to get married.

Robbie's head was spinning as he drove home that night. He liked Amanda, but wasn't this going too fast? They had met barely a week ago, and they were already talking about marriage? Maybe they needed to slow this down.

That's when Robbie got a call from Amanda.

"Hey you! So guess what? My grandparents are gonna be in town in two days. You have to meet them. They'll *love* you. I've already told them all about you and how we feel like we're best friends. I mean, I've shared more with you than any guy before."

The next day Robbie dumped Amanda. No lie.

Men are born to lead. Robbie never got that chance with Amanda. She led almost everything. Amanda was not a bad girl. On the contrary, she was a lovely Christian girl. But at the end of the day, she didn't let Robbie lead the relationship.

She was chasing him. He never got to chase her.

Men are designed to lead, and we crave respect. By not allowing him to lead their relationship, Amanda disrespected Robbie, and she also got her heart broken in the process.

If she had allowed Robbie to take the reins of the relationship, it might have progressed at a more casual pace. They may have still broken up in the end, but at least it would have been after a few dates and not after a whirlwind of a week.

Or maybe they'd still be together because Robbie would feel respected. Guys are attracted to women who let us lead and who respect us.

Ladies, if you try to control a relationship and maneuver it to the speed you want it to go, it will end in heartbreak. Let the guy lead. If he's a godly man, he will honor you and cherish you. He will encourage you to deepen your relationship with Jesus. He will bring out the best in you and want the best for you.

That's the kind of godly guy you want to be with.

If a guy doesn't have the maturity to take charge, then let him go. He may need time to grow up, or he may just not be the guy for you. If you let the guy lead a dating relationship, then you will know pretty quickly whether or not this is the kind of guy you should be dating. It's almost like you get to put him to the test. Will he man up? If not, let him go. Patience pays off. It's not easy, but it's the wise choice for your heart.

On the flip side, a lot of guys lead in a negative way. They pressure girls for sex. They treat girls harshly. These men aren't leading the relationship, they are dominating the relationship. Here's how a godly guy should lead:

> Husbands, you must love your wives so *deeply, purely, and sacrificially that we can understand it only when we* compare it to the love the Anointed One has for *His bride*, the church. (Eph. 5:25 VOICE)

This is what love looks like. A guy should lead and love a girl so well that it mirrors how Jesus (the Anointed One) leads and loves the church.

When a godly guy is leading, the girl is heard and also put first. This isn't some kind of relationship where the guy is the king and the woman must do everything he says. This is a kind of love where a godly man would die for his girl, where he would place his needs second to hers, where the man views her as more valuable than himself.

It's a sacrificial love.

When a girl supports her man and allows him to lead, maturity takes place in them both. A huge change occurred in my life when I started dating Kelsey. I led the relationship because she let me lead it. Ask anyone who knew me before Kelsey, and they will tell you I'm a different man today, and for the better. Kelsey let me lead our relationship, and it made me into the man I am today.

She prayed for me, talked with me, and supported my decisions for us. She also let me do all the firsts in our relationship. I was the one who asked her out on our first date. I was the one who asked her if I could hold her hand. I was the one who initiated our first kiss. I was the one who first said, "I love you." I was the one who first brought up marriage.

I got to be the man and Kelsey got to be the woman, just like God designed.

When the roles get reversed, there is heartbreak involved. I'm a better man because Kelsey is in my life. I tell people the day I truly grew from a boy to a man was the day I decided to pursue Kelsey. If Kelsey had chased me and I never had the opportunity to really pursue her, I would not be the man she needs.

————XO————

DJ, a guy in my high school chemistry class, was dating the most popular girl in school, Ashley. She was very pretty, but she wasn't very nice. Ashley knew she was the most popular girl in school, and she believed she deserved to be.

DJ had been dating Ashley for a few weeks. They'd go to football games and school dances together, and everyone was talking about them. They were *the* couple in school at the time.

When the bell would ring after chemistry class, Ashley would be waiting outside the door for DJ. She would grab his arm and they would walk down the hall as everyone stared at them. It was weird. Somehow they became high school royalty.

One day I walked out of class behind DJ. As usual, Ashley was there ready to greet him. But the greeting didn't go at all like I thought it would.

"DJ!" Ashley fumed as she grabbed his arm.

"What?" he said, completely dumbfounded. I followed close behind because my locker was in the same direction they were headed (and because I was curious why she was so upset).

She looked furious. "Why didn't you call me back last night?"

DJ scrambled to answer her. "Babe, I called you at 11:30. You didn't pick up. Did you get my message?"

"Yeah, I got it," she scoffed. "DJ, I don't care if you had to come in early to retake an exam, you don't go to bed until after you talk to me."

"What? Babe, that's crazy. Of course I wanted to talk to you."

"Shut up, DJ." Ashley stopped in the middle of the hallway. People were looking and could tell they were in a fight. She pointed her finger at his chest. "Maybe you're not ready to actually be a boyfriend." With that, she turned and stormed off.

DJ was humiliated.

He tried to act like it was no big deal, but I could tell that he was hurt. Deeply. I felt bad for the guy. His girlfriend had just made him look like a complete fool in front of everyone.

Why in the world would he continue to date this girl who would consistently belittle him? DJ must have been asking himself the same question, because he had dumped Ashley by lunchtime.

Ladies, affirmation is the key to a guy's heart.

When a man feels built up, it's like he can conquer the world. When you encourage a guy or give him respect for something he did or said, his confidence shoots through the roof. And guys like to be around girls who build them up.

Now, obviously, guys aren't perfect. We mess up. And it's okay to talk to a guy about something he did that hurt you. That's part of being a friend or having a boyfriend.

> Ladies, affirmation is the key to a guy's heart.

But never talk about a guy's mistake in front of other people. That's the quickest way to ruin a friendship, relationship, or marriage. Keep the problem between the two of you.

I remember which girls in high school encouraged me and which girls belittled me. I hung out *way* more with the girls who encouraged me. They got more of my attention and conversation than the other girls, and I think most guys feel the same way.

Nobody wants to feel like they are dumb or underappreciated. What girls say about guys matters to us. A whole lot. So use your words to build guys up.

From Us Both

Here's the big secret on how to treat a guy: respect him. Let him lead. When you do that, you get to see what kind of leader he will be. If your guy isn't leading you in a godly way, then let him go. Be the kind of girl who shows respect and gives away compliments.

NOTE: If someone in your life is abusing you physically, mentally, or emotionally, please tell someone. Contact a Christian adult who can help. God wants you to be in a loving and respectful environment, not a harmful one.

6

What a Girl Wants

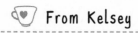 **From Kelsey**

Girls, you need to know that you are a real princess and should always be treated like one. It doesn't matter if you are a girly girl or not; you deserve to be treated with the utmost respect and love. God wants you to know that He not only values you as a person, but He cares about your deepest desires, your hopes and dreams. Your future.

How do I know this? It's in the Bible.

> We are confident that God is able to orchestrate everything to work toward something good *and beautiful* when we love Him and accept His invitation to live according to His plan. (Rom. 8:28 VOICE)

God loves you more than you could ever imagine.

Have you put your trust in God? Have you given Him your whole heart? Giving your whole heart over to God is the greatest thing in the world. He knows what's ahead in your life. He also has the greatest plans for you when you follow His leading.

God says you are worth far more than gold, so shouldn't you think so too?

Sometimes we find ourselves in a situation or in a relationship with a guy we know doesn't treat us like we should be treated. As an example, let me tell you about my friend Emmy.

Emmy was the sweetest, kindest person I knew. No one is perfect, but Emmy was the type of person where it was hard to find a flaw. I met her while I was in high school, but we didn't go to the same school. We met doing theater together. It was late fall heading into winter, and we both auditioned for *Beauty and the Beast*.

Auditions are fun and scary all at the same time. You show up already nervous because you want to be cast so badly and you know you were made for the show. Then you walk into a building where a person is checking you in. You sign in and present your headshot and resume.

I should also add that this entire time the room is quiet. You see some actors who have already signed in. You watch others enter after you. All the while the room feels more silent.

That day I arrived at my audition early enough to sign in and still have time to step outside and get some fresh air. That's when I met Emmy.

We both said hello and commented on how very quiet the room was inside the audition building. She told me about her dance and theater background, and I did the same. We

God cares about your *deepest desires,* your **hopes** and *dreams.*

had a lot in common, and I could tell right away she was a sweet girl. With some girls you can feel "girl games" starting, but not with Emmy. We auditioned, and each of us got a callback for the show.

I was so excited to get a callback. *Beauty and the Beast* is one of my favorite shows, and if I were to be cast we would be performing the entire month of December up until a few days before Christmas. I hadn't done a show during the Christmas season before, but it sounded magical.

Callbacks were long and hard. We all had to learn our dance audition first. Then we gathered around the piano and sang different songs and parts from the show. Emmy was doing great, and I felt like I was too.

A week later the cast list was posted online, and Emmy and I both made the show. I was sad at first because I didn't get cast as Belle, the leading female role. I had sung for the lead at callbacks, but there were so many talented singers who auditioned.

Emmy had also tried out for Belle, but she didn't get the part either. Instead, we were both cast in the ensemble. Although it was a smaller part than I had hoped for, it was still a dream come true to be cast in *Beauty and the Beast*.

Just like that we began rehearsals. Our cast was insanely talented, and I was so honored to be a part of it. One day after rehearsal Emmy asked if I wanted to join her for a cup of tea at a local teahouse.

We grabbed our things, got all bundled up in our winter coats, and were on our way to NW 23rd Street in Portland, Oregon. It's a quaint street that has a perfect mix of Portland culture, cute little boutiques, and fabulous coffee shops and teahouses.

As we drove, Emmy started telling me a little about her family. She loved her parents very much, which I thought was wonderful because sometimes high school kids think it's not cool to love their parents. That was never me; I actually enjoyed spending time with my parents. So I liked that we had that in common.

She had one sister who was married and out of the house. The two of them were still extremely close. Emmy absolutely loved her brother-in-law. He was the type of guy who genuinely cared about Emmy's family. He was funny and smart, and he loved her sister exceptionally well.

Emmy also shared that she hoped her future Prince Charming would be exactly like her brother-in-law. Emmy's sister had met her husband in college, and they had married young. They were finishing up their junior year when he proposed, and the summer after they graduated they were married.

Emmy loved that. I could tell she loved her sister very much, and she loved their love story. Her eyes sparkled as she told me more about her sister and brother-in-law. I couldn't help but smile while she was telling me about their love.

Oh, how I longed for my forever Prince Charming.

At that time I was single and lonely. Very lonely. I had no clue when and where and how my Prince Charming would ever find me, or if he would even show up at all.

My heart melted just thinking about two people so young and so in love with one another. Emmy loved Jesus and shared how her faith was very important to her. That was really encouraging to me. Not only did I not have a boyfriend, but I didn't have many Christian friends in my life. I was so thankful to meet such a sweet friend like Emmy.

When we got to the teahouse, we parked and got out of the car. The street was the perfect winter scene. Every single shop had Christmas decorations and window displays, making it truly the most wonderful time of the year.

We walked toward the teahouse, laughing and taking selfies. The temperature was dropping, but we didn't mind. We walked inside and grabbed a table near the fireplace. It was one of the coolest teahouses, just perfect for any conversation.

I ordered peppermint tea and Emmy ordered a chai. The conversation bounced from our excitement about the show to family. I was fortunate growing up with two parents who loved, cherished, and respected each other.

Emmy and I both smiled at the thought that our parents were still madly in love. Emmy also had the beautiful example of her sister and brother-in-law, so I didn't see the next hour of our conversation coming.

Emmy started telling me about the guy she had been dating for the past year. We had been going through rehearsals together for weeks at that point, and she had never mentioned her boyfriend before.

Emmy told me that while she was comfortable in the relationship, she didn't actually love her boyfriend. And she confessed that he didn't treat her like she felt she should be treated.

She gave me a window into one of their dates. They were driving in the car when she yelled with excitement, "Oh my gosh! I love this song!" then started dancing in her seat and singing along.

Her boyfriend rolled his eyes and said, "You like this dumb pop song? I sometimes just don't get you." Emmy said she felt like she was floating above the car looking down on this horrible yet insightful scene.

She looked over at her boyfriend. "We've been dating for a year now, and this is news to you? I've told you plenty of times about my favorite songs, movies, and books. Sometimes I feel like you aren't really listening."

He gave her a wink and said, "Well, babe, sometimes I don't listen because sometimes your thoughts and your likes are boring. But don't worry, I still love ya!"

My heart sank. Even though the story she shared was only about a song, I could tell that she was deeply hurt. This story was just one of many. I mean, Emmy was amazing and deserved nothing but the very best. She could feel God prompting her to break up with this guy, but she didn't want to be alone.

She looked defeated over the entire relationship with her boyfriend. I urged her to really pray and see if maybe she would be better off without him. She agreed. She knew deep down he was not the one.

You deserve nothing but the very best when it comes to boys. Protect your heart.

The conversation turned back to lighter topics at that point, but Emmy's story was still running through my head. No matter how attached or comfortable I felt with a guy, if he was the wrong guy for me I would never want to just settle and stay with him. Time is too precious. And we only get this one life.

Girls, don't fill your days with dating the wrong guy.

If he puts you down, makes fun of you, or just doesn't understand your heart . . . please let him go. It may hurt in the beginning, but you deserve nothing but the very best when it comes to boys. Protect your heart.

----xo----

We've all been on horrible dates, right? Oh, you haven't? Yeah, me neither.

Wait. Real talk . . . I totally have. Going on a date can be so much fun, or it can be an utter disaster.

At one point in my life there was this guy who was super cute. We met in college. We saw each other in the library, and that's where it all started.

We had some friends in common, and our conversation seemed to really flow effortlessly. He had the build of a football player. I didn't get much studying done that day, but seeing how comfortable and fun our conversation was, I hoped that wouldn't be our only meeting.

The next day we saw each other in the parking lot. Our cars were parked right next to each other. We both laughed, and I could feel the chemistry starting to grow between us. He smiled and said, "Well, it looks like even our cars want us to hang out. Are you free tonight for ice cream?"

I was definitely already liking this day. Cute boy, sweet smile, and we had friends in common, so I knew he wasn't a total creep. And now he was asking me out on an ice cream date. Umm . . . yeah, that sounded fun!

We decided to meet on campus at 7:30 p.m. Our school had the best ice cream shop, plus I felt safer not driving with him right away.

It was 7:25 when I walked in. I'm not one to run early, and this is something I'm desperately trying to work on. But that night I was so proud of myself for showing up five whole minutes early. I got in line and looked around to see if he was there yet.

I finally caught a glimpse of him flirting with another girl in the corner. They were laughing and her hand kept inching closer and closer to his hand on the table. Excuse me? This was the sweet, funny, kind (so I thought) guy I was meeting for ice cream?

I thought there must be some explanation for this absurd scene playing out right before my eyes. I quickly walked over to them. He stood right away and introduced me to the girl.

The girl got up, hugged him goodbye, and left. He smiled and said, "You must be wondering who that girl was?"

"Yes, I am," I said, a tad bit mean and sarcastic.

"She's my ex-girlfriend, but we're just friends."

Well, that explains all of the flirting and touching. "I see. Yeah, you two looked super uncomfortable with each other." I laughed with a hint of sarcasm. Our first date had certainly started off with a bang.

With that opening behind us, my date started talking about how much he bench-pressed this week. He told me he was trying to increase his muscle mass for next season. He then went into this long monologue about how he was voted MVP on his football team for all four years in high school. He started to explain what MVP meant.

"You see, MVP stands for most valuable—"

"Yes, I know." I smiled, cutting him off. By this point, I was annoyed. *What happened to the kind, relaxed, fun guy I met at the library?*

I was looking across the table at this guy, trying to look engaged in the conversation, when he suddenly stopped talking. To that point he hadn't asked me a single question. He had just gone on and on about himself. So this is when I naturally thought he would finally ask me something . . . anything.

Nope. Instead, he reached down into his Nike backpack and said, "You know what, I actually have to take this call. It's my ex-girlfriend, and she probably has a question about our project for English."

The room was spinning and my heart felt extremely confused. I faintly smiled, exhausted from the evening, and said, "Yeah, totally take the call." While he was still talking to his ex-girlfriend, I quickly gathered my things, waved goodbye to him, and darted for the door.

Worst first date ever. My mind really was blown.

That night in my dorm room, I sat on my bed and grabbed my journal. I wrote something I'll never forget. At the top of the page I wrote "What a girl wants."

I wrote about what I wanted in a guy, in a first date, and in a boyfriend. I told myself I should be valued, cherished, and respected. And I reminded myself that I should never settle for anything less.

When I had met that cute, nice guy at the library, I couldn't have known he would turn out to be my worst first date ever. I took a chance and went on the date. And it didn't work out.

We need to take chances and risks in life, so sure, go on the date. But don't for a second forget how valuable you are to God. God sees you, He knows your heart, and He wants you to be treated the very best.

Oh, and if you do go on a bad first date, or a bad date in general . . . go home after it's over and journal all of the details. You may be crying at first like I was, but trust me, you'll be laughing later.

From Kyle

When Kelsey and I first got married, we started volunteering at church with the high school youth group. It was an absolute blast. The youth pastor organized concerts and black light dance parties, and we had great speakers and deep talks. We grew close to the students and loved hanging with them.

One girl in particular got really close to Kelsey. Her name was Courtney. She graduated from high school in the spring and was now off beginning her first semester at college. One day she called Kelsey.

"Hey! How are you?" Kelsey asked. "I've got Kyle here too, so you're on speakerphone."

"Hey Courtney," I said.

"Hey guys! I'm doing great. Having a fun time and meeting some good friends. I'm about to step into my next class, but I can't wait to tell you more about it all."

"Well, I'd love to grab coffee and hear about it when you're back in town next," Kelsey said.

"Sounds perfect. Oh, and something kind of unexpected happened as well. I found a great guy!"

Kelsey got all the details. Courtney met this guy in her psychology class, but he was from Nashville like her. He went to a church across town. They ended up working together on a class project, and now they had just started dating. His name was Garrett.

He sounded like a great guy. I knew Courtney had a strong relationship with God, so I assumed Garrett's relationship with God was pretty strong as well. Kelsey and I wanted a guy for Courtney who truly loved God and who truly loved her.

Kelsey followed Courtney and Garrett through social media. Courtney posted about him all the time, and they seemed really happy. From what Courtney consistently posted, it seemed like Garrett was a strong leader.

Later that fall, our youth group organized a reunion dance party for all the seniors who went away to college. We planned it during their college fall break.

Courtney called Kelsey when she got the invite for the reunion. "Perfect! It's gonna be such a fun night. And you all will get to meet Garrett," she squealed.

The reunion dance arrived with the brisk cool air of late fall. As Kelsey and I made our way up the front steps of the building, a blonde girl ran past us giggling. She was quickly followed by a built guy who was laughing as hard as she was. He grabbed her waist to tickle her.

"Stop! Stop!" she playfully screamed. "Stop it, Garrett."

Garrett?

Surely this must be another guy named Garrett. It's a popular name for guys, I suppose. *How weird, though*, I thought to myself. From the back, his dark hair looked pretty similar to Courtney's Garrett. Couldn't be, though. Couldn't be.

We went inside and were greeted by tons of familiar faces. The night was awesome. We got to see students we hadn't seen in months. We got to hear about their school, their friends, and how their relationship with God was going.

Courtney saw us from across the room and ran over. "Hey!" she yelled as she gave us both a hug. "It's so good to see you!"

"I know." Kelsey beamed. "I keep smiling looking around this room."

"Oh my gosh, I want to introduce you to Garrett," Courtney gushed. "Hold on a sec."

She turned and made her way across the dance floor. I saw her stop and grab a guy's hand. He had the same dark hair as the guy I had seen on the steps. As they walked closer, I could see that this *was* the guy from earlier.

The guy who had been flirting with the blonde.

Courtney smiled widely as she turned the corner. I smiled back, trying not to show my hesitation.

"Kyle and Kelsey, this is Garrett."

I stuck out my hand to shake his. "Hey man."

"Hi," he replied with a full smile.

"Courtney's told us a lot about you," I said.

"Oh cool!" he said, nodding. He turned to Courtney. "Babe, I'm going to get some more water. I'll be back." He gave a full smile again and walked away.

"Okay. I'll miss you."

And then Garrett was gone. I tried to contain my dislike of Garrett the best I could for the next few minutes. Courtney obviously really liked the guy and wanted us to like him as well. Any red flags we had about him weren't appropriate to share at this moment, even though I wanted so badly to tell her what I had seen on the steps. Garrett seemed to be a charmer and a flirt, but it would have to wait. At least until after the reunion. Now was a time of celebration.

The DJ was playing banging music while tons of students packed the dance floor. Kelsey and I made our way to the middle of the dance floor to join the students and other youth leaders. After a few songs, Courtney left, saying that she was going to get Garrett. We watched as she maneuvered her way off the dance floor.

We saw her find Garrett at one of the back tables where he sat with some other students. They were laughing loudly. I noticed the blonde girl from the steps was at the table as well.

Courtney walked up and put her hand on Garrett's shoulder. He turned to look up at her and nodded "Hey," then returned his attention to the others at the table and began laughing at something one of them said. Courtney tapped his shoulder again and motioned for him to follow her, and I saw him get up reluctantly.

They walked a good distance away from the table. Courtney began to talk, and I could see Garrett shaking his head. He did not want to get up and go be with her. His arm motions made it clear that he wanted to stay where he was.

I was shocked. It was hard for me to believe Garrett wouldn't come and at least stand by the dance floor with her. It was clear he'd rather be hanging with the people at the table.

Courtney was obviously upset and took a step away from Garrett. We watched as he moved forward and put his arms around her. He kept holding her until she gave a faint smile. He kissed her and then returned to his friends.

Courtney walked slowly back to the dance floor. When she finally rejoined us, I could tell she was faking a smile.

"Where's Garrett?" Kelsey asked. "Is he gonna join us?"

"Oh, Garrett has some friends that are here right now," Courtney replied, acting like it was no big deal. "He'll catch up with us later."

"Oh, okay."

Courtney loved spending time with people. Time was one of her love languages. So for Garrett not to spend time with her when he was her guest to this event said quite a lot about their relationship.

This Garrett did not match up with the Garrett we saw and read about on Courtney's posts. She had made him out to be some Prince Charming. And he was charming. But he definitely didn't treat her like his princess.

It turns out Kelsey and I weren't the only people who saw Garrett flirting with another girl. One of Courtney's friends had seen it as well and told her about it. As people began getting their coats and heading home for the night, Courtney and Garrett got into a heated argument and left separately.

Kelsey didn't hear from Courtney for a few weeks after that, but when she finally did, Courtney had some news to share.

"Garrett and I broke up."

"Oh, Courtney . . . I'm sorry," Kelsey said with a sigh.

Courtney took a deep breath and said, "I'm pretty hurt. I so badly wanted him to be my guy."

"I know you did."

A few moments of silence went by and then Kelsey said, "But to be honest, Court, you deserve better."

"Thanks. I mean, he was cute and fun, but I know he didn't have much of a relationship with God. I was the one texting him Bible verses here and there and bringing up God."

"There's an amazing guy for you, Courtney. I know it," Kelsey said strongly. "Wait for him. Don't settle for the Garretts."

"Ha!" she laughed. "I think I'm done with the Garretts . . . forever."

"You deserve more."

"I know that now," she replied.

For the next year, Courtney was single. And single on purpose. She could have gotten a boyfriend if she wanted, but she was waiting. Waiting for a different kind of guy.

She didn't want another Garrett.

A year after Garrett and Courtney broke up, she started dating a guy named Jeremy. From what we could see on Instagram, he seemed like a great guy. He posted about football, his friends, and also his favorite Bible verses. Courtney looked really happy with him. But I remembered that she had also looked really happy with Garrett.

A few months after they got together, Courtney left on a mission trip to Guatemala. While she was gone, Jeremy contacted her mom and asked if it would be okay to leave a surprise in Courtney's bedroom for when she returned.

When Courtney came home and saw her surprise, she couldn't believe it. Jeremy had taped small note cards all over her room. One over her bed, one on her bathroom mirror, one on her door, one over the window. On the cards were prayers for Courtney. Messages like,

On the notecard over her bed: "Dear God, help Courtney feel Your love and presence as she falls asleep tonight. Watch over her and protect her."

On the notecard by her door: "Help Courtney love the people You've placed in her life today, just like You have loved her."

Courtney was overwhelmed. And that was only one of the many stories I heard about Jeremy's love for her. Jeremy treated Courtney like a princess. Courtney kept those notecards on her bedroom wall the entire time they dated.

In fact, she didn't take those precious notes down until she was packing up her room and preparing to move into the apartment she and Jeremy had found for after their wedding. She still has them in a special box in their home today.

Jeremy cared about Courtney's heart, her needs, and her relationship with God. He led the relationship spiritually. He gave Courtney exactly what a girl wants.

> Husbands, go all out in your love for your wives, exactly as Christ did for the church—a love marked by giving, not getting. Christ's love makes the church whole. His words evoke her beauty. Everything he does and says is designed to bring the best out of her, dressing her in dazzling white silk, radiant with holiness. And that is how husbands ought to love their wives. (Eph. 5:25–28 Message)

Ladies, this is how a guy should treat you. This verse says a guy should "go all out" in his love for you. You are a prized jewel, a treasure that God created with His own hands. Any guy who wants to date or marry you should know that and show that with his actions. Wait for the guy who leads you in love and leads you spiritually.

Wait for the guy who leads you in love and leads you spiritually.

From Us Both

What do you want in a relationship?

You want the best. You want true love. Look for a guy who displays God's love to you. Who chases after God. Who loves sacrificially. Who treasures you. God wouldn't want anything less for you.

7

Worth the Wait

From Kelsey

Kyle and I had a beautiful wedding. It honestly was the wedding of my dreams. After it was all over, we walked down a cobblestone path with our family and friends on either side and headed into our new life together. Kyle surprised me by arranging a beautiful vintage getaway car.

The moment we drove away, my heart began to soar. Our first night together as husband and wife was magical. The next morning came early, and then we were off on our honeymoon.

Let me tell you something: *sex is worth waiting for.* I don't mean to make you feel uncomfortable, I just want to be straight-up honest.

God created sex to be between a husband and wife. And Kyle and I both saved ourselves for one another, meaning that night after our wedding was our first time having sex. Was it difficult to wait? Of course. But in God's strength we both waited, and it was worth it!

What did it take to get to that point? It all started with a commitment each of us had made more than a decade earlier.

----xo----

Let me take you back to the morning of my thirteenth birthday. It was a beautiful morning, and I just knew it was going to be the best day ever, because after all, it was my thirteenth birthday! I remember my mom smiling so big as I came down the stairs that morning. She was in the kitchen making me my favorite breakfast: eggs and toast.

My dad and brothers came in from the other room and shouted, "Happy birthday!" Covering the kitchen countertop were beautiful cards that all had the number thirteen on them. I also spotted some stunningly wrapped presents scattered about. I couldn't believe I was actually thirteen years old.

Over the years leading up to that day, my parents had talked to me about being pure and saving myself for my husband. But I never really understood what all that meant until that day, my thirteenth birthday.

That morning was perfect, and the rest of the day was going to be just as wonderful. My mom told me that she and my dad were going to take me out for a special date. I've always loved getting dressed up and going places, especially on my birthday. So I sprinted up the stairs to choose my birthday outfit.

It was finally time to leave for the surprise date with my parents. We spent the drive talking about friends and boys and life. I loved talking to my parents, and I still do.

We pulled up to this beautiful spot at the waterfront by the Columbia River, which was one of my favorite places to go in Washington. It has a gorgeous walking path that stretches along the river. You can also see the city of Portland, Oregon, on the other side.

Dad parked the car. We all got out and started to walk. I was very excited because going on a walk is one of my favorite things to do. Going for walks and having deep talks with the people I love makes my heart so happy. And that moment, walking alongside the river with my parents, did just that.

As we approached a bench, my dad motioned for the three of us to sit down. My parents told me they had a big surprise present for me. They took hold of my hands and began praying with me.

The prayer talked about purity: what it means to be pure before the Lord, how we can stay pure, how I should save sex for my future husband. It was one of the most beautiful prayers ever.

After it was over, they pulled out a tiny box that could only have one thing inside it. A ring! It was a purity ring. I was so excited not only to wear this beautiful ring but to really follow through with the meaning behind it. My heart felt so close to Jesus in that moment, and I never wanted that day to end.

My parents also presented me with a beautifully designed document. It was a purity contract they printed on vintage paper. I signed my name, stating that I would remain pure for my future husband. They signed it, stating they would stand by me.

As we continued our walk down the waterfront with the sun starting to set, I said a little prayer for my future husband.

I had no clue who he was or where he lived, but I knew one thing: I knew he was really out there. I also knew I could pray for him right then and there. So I did.

My thirteenth birthday will always stay with me. I got a beautiful purity ring from my parents as well as some other great presents. But what I remember the most was praying for my future husband and telling God in my prayer that I was going to save myself for that boy—that I would wait for him every single day no matter how long it took until the two of us were married.

I share that story with you because purity is a big deal. God wants all of us to be pure before Him. This story is not supposed to make you feel guilty. Rather, I want it to give you hope and encouragement.

I'm not sure what you are going through or where you stand on purity, but I do know this: God loves you so much. If you believe in Him, He calls you His own.

You may be someone who gave yourself away physically before marriage, and you know it was wrong according to God's Word. But guess what? God never stopped loving you. He never will.

If you are that person, please make this the day when you commit to start again. It's never too late to say you're sorry to God. He knows everything about you, and He loves you anyway.

How do I know? Because God sees my sins and loves me anyway.

I'm a very physical person, and purity was a challenge for me, especially when I had a boyfriend. Only in God's strength was I able to keep the promise I made on my thirteenth birthday.

We must never forget that God loves us all the time, no matter how we fail. So start over today. Simply tell God you're sorry for the things you've done in the past and ask Him to give you a clean and fresh heart.

We all mess up, but when we repent and tell God we're sorry, we are wiped clean. We are *pure* before his eyes.

Today can be a brand-new start. If, however, you have remained committed to saving yourself for your future husband, then I want to encourage you to hang in there. Stay connected with friends who love Jesus. Give whatever you're feeling over to God. No matter what our sin struggle is, God loves us. But He also loves purity, and He wants us to save sex for marriage.

Chase after God. Let Him come into your heart and work in your life. You will see that when you live for God, when you chase Him, *He* will help you live a pure lifestyle.

----XO----

My friend Lily learned about sex the hard way. It was our junior year of high school and Lily started dating Connor, a guy on the basketball team. Lily told me she really liked this boy but she wasn't willing to compromise her convictions on purity.

At the beginning of their relationship, Connor would hold open the car door when they went on a date and bring her flowers for no reason. He seemed perfectly willing to get to know her heart and not her body. Lily called him a gentleman. He seemed like a pretty good guy.

But it was only a matter of time before Connor revealed his true colors.

After two months of dating, Connor started pressuring Lily to go further than she wanted to physically. Then things got serious very quickly.

After their sixth-month anniversary, Lily came to me and shared that she had slept with Connor. With tears streaming down her face, she also told me that he had treated her differently ever since.

Lily broke up with him after only a few more weeks. Why? Because she found out Connor was cheating on her with another girl from a different school. It was crazy how distant Connor became. Suddenly he started being mean to Lily and making little jokes at her expense in front of his guy friends.

In no time, the whole school found out Connor had been cheating on Lily. Let's just say many tears were shed. My heart hurt for her. I hated seeing Lily cry, but her feelings were real, and she couldn't hide the fact that she was embarrassed, depressed, scared, and heartbroken.

The year went on, and I spent a lot of time with Lily. Eventually she started coming to church with me. We would pray a lot together. We would sit and have wonderful, deep, emotional talks about her broken heart, the one she was still living with every single day.

By God's grace and unfailing love my friend gave her heart fully over to Jesus, and she felt that hole in her heart go away. After a long time of hurting, questioning, tears, and anger, Jesus healed my friend's heart.

Lily's broken heart was glued back together by God. Please learn from her story. Learn from the brokenness and shame she felt. God never wants *you* to feel this way. In Him, there is forgiveness and a new day. A fresh beginning. Through the power of Jesus, my friend experienced God's love, grace, and forgiveness.

But the best choice is to avoid the heartbreak from the start. Chase after Jesus instead of guys. Remember, He knows the plans He has for you, and they are the best plans.

Do you trust God with your happily ever after? Your story is uniquely yours. If you chase after God, you have a bright future ahead.

Please save yourself. Not just your heart, but your purity. Your friends and some guys will make you feel like you're the only one your age who hasn't had sex. That isn't true.

You're not alone.

----XO----

When I was a freshman in high school, I had a friend who was a few years older than me. I looked up to her and wanted to be just like her. She was sweet, funny, pretty, and she loved the Lord.

We would have coffee once every two weeks, and I always looked forward to hanging out with her. She also had the cutest boyfriend, and they both went to my church. We were all in the same youth group.

We are going to mess up, but *it's what we learn* from those mistakes *that really counts.*

One day while we were out for coffee, she told me that she was pregnant. My heart stopped. The noise of the coffee shop disappeared, and all I could hear was the pounding of my own heartbeat. I literally thought she started speaking in another language. I couldn't believe what I had just heard.

How could this be?

I had looked up to this friend so much, and she had helped me grow closer to God. She gave the best advice and had always told me that she and her boyfriend were committed to waiting until marriage to have sex. Now here we were, and she had just told me she was pregnant.

I was completely devastated, and she wasn't too happy either. With tears streaming down her face, she looked at me and said, "I'm so sorry, Kels. I know you are disappointed in me, and you have every right to be."

I couldn't really talk. When I thought about responding my throat closed with sorrow. I could feel the tears starting to well up inside. The car ride home together was quiet, very quiet.

She dropped me off at my house, and as her car pulled out of the driveway, I started to cry . . . hard.

Lord, how could this be true? I searched the sky for some kind of answer. Right about that time my mom came outside. She could tell I was crying and very upset. We both sat down and she held me while tears spilled down my cheeks.

My friend ended up being homeschooled the rest of the year. She went around to different high schools and youth groups talking about teen pregnancy and how heartbreaking it is. She realized in talking about it that she found healing and forgiveness from God.

Jesus still loved her *so* much.

I was very young at the time, and after the shock wore off, I told my friend I was sorry. Sorry for my initial reaction and sorry for not being there for her. Nobody's perfect, but when you're growing up it's sometimes easy to think the people who are older than you *are* perfect.

Girls, if you are thinking about giving away your virginity . . . don't. You will not only hurt yourself, but you will hurt those around you. Someone is looking to *you* right now. You have the chance to be a leader and an example for someone younger or older than you.

We are going to mess up, but it's what we learn from those mistakes that really counts.

----xo----

My prayer is that this chapter has encouraged you to remain pure. To keep chasing after God and to save yourself for your future husband. Or maybe this chapter has helped heal your heart and reminded you that God loves you and forgives you for anything you've done in the past.

Maybe you were encouraged to start over today.

If you have a Christian woman who is a mentor in your life (your mom, aunt, sister, teacher, youth group leader) go talk to her. For me, it was my mom. I shared everything with her. And I'm so glad I did.

Share with your mentor what's on your heart. She loves you, and I know she cares about all aspects of your life. Even when it feels awkward, just give her grace. Talk about sex with her. It's so important to not keep it all inside.

Maybe now you want to go write a letter to your future husband. Tell him how much you love him, that you're praying for him, and that you're saving yourself for him no matter what.

Once you're married, *then* go have sex with your husband. God created sex, and it's a beautiful, wonderful, amazing thing in marriage!

 ## From Kyle

Let me start by saying sex *is* worth the wait. I didn't have sex until I was married at twenty-three years old, and wow, was it ever worth waiting for! Sex is *amazing*. It truly bonds you soul to soul with someone. God designed it that way.

But He designed it for a specific purpose: as a gift for a husband and wife and as the way to create a family. And like with most things in life, if not used properly, there are unfortunate consequences.

If someone gives you a map and you don't follow it correctly, you'll get lost. If someone gives you a car and you crash it, the car will be damaged.

In marriage, sex works perfectly. Engaging in sex outside of marriage, well . . . you can count on getting hurt.

During my summer break from college, I hung out with some friends from my hometown. We would try to do something fun almost every weekend. One of my closest friends was a guy named Ethan.

One night, we went out to listen to some live music. A girl was playing her set that night. She had a cool jazzy voice. Her name was Summer. Right away I could tell Ethan was enamored with her.

"Could you be staring at that girl any harder, dude?" I asked with a laugh.

"Huh?" he said, not moving his eyes from Summer. "Oh . . . sorry," he replied as he shook his head side to side like he was coming out of a trance.

"Seems like you really like her music." I smiled.

"Her music . . . her face . . . her eyes . . ."

"Wow." I rolled my eyes and laughed.

After her set was finished, Ethan made his way up to the front and introduced himself to Summer. They talked for a few minutes, and even from where I was sitting I could tell they had plenty of chemistry. Summer must have been as into Ethan as he was into her.

He made his way to the seat beside me and said with a happy look, "She's awesome."

"Oh good!" I replied.

"And she just started going to our church."

"That is awesome."

"We exchanged numbers," Ethan said as he sat down in his seat with a smirk. "I'll call her tomorrow."

And Ethan did just that. After a few more group hangouts, they began dating. They were both a lot of fun to be around, and everyone thought they made a cute couple.

If there were any red flags to the start of the relationship, it was that they seemed to be pretty physical right away. Her hand high on his leg. His arms wrapped tightly around her. They were always kind of "glued" together.

I don't have a problem with public displays of affection. If you ever see Kelsey and me out and about, you'll probably see just that. But something was different with them. Things seemed to be heating up fast.

August came and our group of friends decided to take a road trip a few hours to the Jersey shore. A friend of ours and his parents were letting us stay at their beach house. I had gone to the Jersey shore with my family almost every year growing up. I loved it there.

Ethan had to work the day our group was leaving, so he told us he would meet us down there the next afternoon. We arrived at the beach and it was magnificent. Soft sand, blue sky, nice waves . . . a little taste of paradise. The next afternoon a knock came at the door. It was Ethan and Summer.

"Hey guys!"

"Hey." They both smiled back.

"I can't wait to see the beach!" Summer said.

"Well, come on in." I moved back and gestured inside. "The girls are upstairs and the guys are downstairs."

"Okay, great," Summer said. "Babe, I'm gonna go change." Summer smiled at Ethan and then walked up the stairs.

I looked at Ethan, who appeared exhausted. "You tired, man?"

Ethan looked down. "So tired. We stayed up way too late watching movies last night." He turned to look at me. "Hey, where's the bathroom?"

"Down the hall to the left."

Ethan walked down the hall and turned. He seemed a little off. I had a feeling something had happened. Regardless, I didn't press it. If he wanted to tell me something, he would when he was ready. And maybe everything was fine.

The beach week was an absolute blast. We made so many fun memories. But I did notice that Ethan and Summer were different that week. They weren't as close as usual.

She would hang out with the girls most of the time, and Ethan would hang out with us guys. They were usually inseparable.

A day after we got back, Ethan told me they broke up on the way home from the beach.

"Oh dude, I'm sorry," I said, trying to read his face. "What happened?"

He hesitated, like he was trying to figure out whether or not he wanted to tell a secret.

"A lot happened," he finally admitted. "Not stuff I'm proud of."

I let silence fill the space, waiting to hear what he would say next.

"We moved too fast." The words spilled out of his mouth. "That day you guys were leaving for the beach, I got off work early. So I thought it would be fun to head over to Summer's apartment and surprise her with dinner."

"Okay." I nodded along.

"I picked up some food and went over to her place. We had a good time together watching movies and stuff, but then it got late . . ."

I knew where this was going. My heart already hurt for Ethan.

"And yeah . . . we had sex," he said. The words dropped out of his mouth like a bomb. "We didn't plan on it, but we didn't go out of our way to prevent it," he said, hanging his head. "It just happened. And now everything is different."

I wanted somehow to help, but I realized I couldn't. I could only listen to a hurting friend.

Ethan went on. "It got real bad by the end of the beach week. We didn't want to be around each other because it reminded

us of what we did. It felt like we wouldn't be the same again
. . . at least not together."

Ethan had a lot of regret. He knew one day he would have to tell his wife about this and that he didn't save himself for her.

If you can relate to Ethan's story in any way, hear this and believe it: your story is not over.

God offers grace and forgiveness beyond measure. We don't deserve it, but He grants it freely.

> *Your story is not over. God offers grace and forgiveness beyond measure.*

All it takes is for us to acknowledge that we messed up, that we are broken, and that we desperately need His help and forgiveness.

Jesus died on a cross so that our broken lives can be made beautiful.

Let these verses of truth wash over you:

> If we own up to our sins, God shows that He is faithful and just by forgiving us of our sins and purifying us from the pollution of all the bad things we have done. (1 John 1:9 VOICE)

> He has removed our sins as far from us as the east is from the west. (Ps. 103:12 NLT)

> Anyone who belongs to Christ has become a new person. The old life is gone; a new life has begun! (2 Cor. 5:17 NLT)

These are promises from God. Your story is just beginning.

You can choose today to start again. You can still find your happily ever after with God's guidance. We all have to live with the consequences of our actions, but God is right there helping us. What Satan planned to use for bad in our lives, God can use for good.

So start your new walk of purity today. It's never too late.

Today Ethan is happily married to a girl who loves Jesus. After he confessed his failures to God, he went on quite the journey. Forgiveness and healing followed. He made changes in his life. He had hard conversations. God was faithful through it all, and now Ethan is deeply in love.

If your story isn't like Ethan's and you've kept yourself pure, I encourage you to stick with it. Wait. Wait until you are married to have sex. People today would say that advice sounds ancient and crazy, but it's the best advice I can give to you. It's the way God designed sex. He designed this amazing and passionate expression of love to exist between a man and woman in marriage. Having sex when you're married honors God—after all, it was His idea!

But sex outside of marriage is destructive. First Corinthians 6:18 says, "Run from sexual sin! No other sin so clearly affects the body as this one does. For sexual immorality is a sin against your own body."

I know your high school friends, every movie you watch, and every song you listen to act like sex is no big deal, but the stakes couldn't be higher. I can't emphasize that enough.

Sex is serious.

Waiting for sex is acting in your own best interest. The world says do it now, but I promise you will be happiest if you wait. Choosing purity isn't just what God commands us to do; it's what *is* actually best for us. Choosing purity will lead to success in this life.

Think about it: purity allows you to be free from disease and free from teen pregnancy, and it lays the groundwork for a wonderful and committed marriage. Impurity is risky and the consequences are severe.

God gives us options. He has placed inside of us a free will. You get to make the choice. Not your parents, not your friends, not even God—you get to make the choice.

----xo----

So you want to live sexually pure until marriage? Awesome! Now you must live intentionally. That means taking actions and precautions before something happens and you make a choice you end up regretting. That means chasing after God.

When Kelsey and I started dating, we talked about this. We both wanted to stay pure in our dating relationship until marriage. And boy, it's hard. We both had done things in our past that we wished we hadn't, but with God's strength and guidance, we made it to our wedding as virgins. It can be done. It's not impossible.

Ladies, don't be alone with your boyfriend in his room and don't invite him to your room alone. Go home before things start to escalate physically. Don't watch that R-rated movie with nudity even if everyone around you has seen it. Choose TV programs where casual sex isn't celebrated. Avoid the romance novels that lead your mind to lust.

Be intentional.

----xo----

When I was in middle school, I made a promise in my heart to my future wife. I attended youth group at my church, and one night the leaders gave us an opportunity to write down on a card that we would wait for our future spouse and not have sex before marriage. I signed that document that night.

I held on to that commitment for years. It was a commitment to God and to my future wife. It was a promise that I held on to during difficult times. That same night I wrote the following letter to my future wife:

Dear Love,

I can't wait to meet you. I've waited all these years anxiously for you. I pray for you every night. You're everything to me. I wake up in the morning longing for you. I will love you now and forever. I may not meet you for many years to come, but I'll be thinking of you every day. I long for you, love you, cherish you, and adore you now and forever. Thank you for coming into my life. I thank God for you!

Love,
Your husband, Kyle

I wrote that when I was just thirteen years old. Seriously. Clearly my romantic side bloomed early.

The Christmas after Kelsey and I got engaged, I gave her this letter as a present. It was the best present I have ever given her. I told Kelsey I had prayed for her for years, but to present her with proof—a letter I wrote nearly a decade before meeting her—melted her heart and displayed God's faithfulness.

Today that letter hangs in our living room.

Kelsey also waited for me. She signed a similar purity commitment when she was thirteen. (She already told you that story herself.) The night of our wedding was the first time either of us had sex. And the fact that we hadn't had sex before didn't make the night awkward or scary. Our purity only made sex more amazing because we were sharing this incredible experience together.

Sex is a gift. A gift worth waiting for.

I challenge you to wait. You won't regret it.

From Us Both

Sex is a gift. A gift worth waiting for. Remember, if you've gone too far, choose this moment right now to ask God for forgiveness and start over. God sees all of our mistakes and He loves us more than anyone else could. You are worth the wait and your dream guy is worth waiting for. We believe in you!

8

The Climb

☕ From Kelsey

I was sitting in my room, feeling absolutely alone. Feeling like no guy would ever like me. It was the summer before my sophomore year of high school. By this point I had already had one boyfriend, but the relationship didn't last. I just wanted to be with a guy who could really understand my heart.

I remember sitting on my couch, staring out the window, wondering where he was. Where was this great guy I had been dreaming about my whole life? Where was my dream guy?

It may sound like a sad, lonely picture, but I'm just being real with you. I've had a wonderfully happy life, but there were definitely moments where my heart was so very lonely. And because I feel things so deeply, my heart had been broken one too many times.

So there I was on my couch one night when I started to pray. While looking out the window I asked God the questions that had been inside my heart. "Lord, where is he? Why does it feel like forever until he is here with me, taking me out on a date?" I was up in my room for hours that evening.

I think we need moments like that, at least I do. I need moments to stop, reflect, ask questions, and really cry out to Jesus. God made something very clear to me that night. He gave my heart something to hold on to.

He reminded me that He had a plan for my life and that I could trust Him. Therefore I had to wait, wait, and wait some more until that special guy was revealed to me. I sat there sort of arguing, "God, I am getting a little tired of waiting and waiting for him. Can't he just come now?"

I had to wait, wait, and wait some more until that special guy was revealed to me.

But I also remember feeling God's love and patience wash over me in that moment. It amazes me that God is so patient with us. And because He is so patient, I knew that I had to continue being patient as well, even though my loneliness was very real.

We called this chapter "The Climb" because in this world we will face trials of many kinds. Life will present us with many mountains.

Some mountains will seem so big that we don't even know how we'll begin to climb them. Other trials will feel more like hills. But either way, we'll all have times where we feel alone and hurting.

I want to encourage you that Jesus has overcome the world, and He personally knows your heart. Sometimes God lets us face "mountains" or really difficult times to see how we will react to them. Will we fade away because they are too scary or too hard, or will we chase after Him?

He wants you to see a mountain and say, "Yeah, in God's strength I can totally climb that!"

~~~~xo~~~~

Summer had ended, and I was finally a sophomore in high school. High school for me was sort of measured in events, cheering for our football team, going to all of the basketball games, and lots of school dances. My school had many fun dances where having a date wasn't required.

But there were some dances where having a date mattered—winter formal was one of those. Winter formal was special because everyone had to dress in formal attire, and I loved seeing everyone all dressed up.

But a date needed to be part of the equation.

Before the neon dance my freshman year, I was majorly stressing about having a date, then at the last minute I was asked. I would have preferred not to be asked at the last minute again, but I refused to think no one would ask me to winter formal.

The dance was fast approaching, and of course all of us girls were so excited to see who was going to ask who. It's funny how right before a dance we would all spend extra time getting ready in the morning. I'm not a morning person at all, but every day leading up to winter formal I was up early getting my hair and makeup just right.

At this point the dance was three weeks away, and I still hadn't been asked. I felt okay about it because there were still three whole weeks left. Three weeks of waking up extra early to try and impress the guys at my school. *I've got a few more weeks. It will happen*, I reminded myself each morning.

Before you know it, three weeks turned into two weeks and then one. Then one week turned into two days before the dance. I couldn't believe it. All of my friends had already been asked. And I mean *all* of them. Every guy I had hoped would ask me had now asked someone else, and with every passing day my heart broke a little bit more. I felt like a complete loser.

Soon it was Friday and the dance was the very next day. I woke up that morning thinking surely this was the day when I would finally be asked. I went through the entire day listening to all of my friends talk about their dresses, where they were going to get their nails done, and whose house they would be at for the after party. Let me tell you, that Friday was not a highlight for me.

I felt so left out.

The bell rang, and as I slowly walked out of the building, it really hit me. Not one guy thought of me. Not one guy wanted to call me his date. I wasn't going to my winter formal. I had never felt so alone.

When I got home, I went straight to my mom's room where she was writing that day. I just sat and cried in her arms.

My mom held me and said, "Kels, you have no idea what God has ahead for you. You have to know that your one-in-a-million guy is out there somewhere, and he's waiting for you too. You need to trust Jesus with the timing of this, and when the time is right, you and your Prince Charming will finally be together."

I appreciated every kind and encouraging word my mom said to me in that moment, but it didn't change the fact that I was lonely and without a date to the winter formal.

When you feel alone and neglected by others—especially by a guy—the heartache can feel overwhelming. I don't know if you've ever felt this way, and I'm not even sure where you are in your story. But I'm sure you've experienced some form of heartache, whether it was small or big.

In life we all face mountains that often seem so very large. And sometimes they really are. But guess what? You don't have to climb those mountains alone. God is right there with you. He is helping you up when you fall. He's guiding you when you get lost. My prayer is that this will comfort you.

Sitting at my house alone on a Saturday night while all my friends were out at winter formal was hard. Waking up and realizing, "Oh, today is Valentine's Day and I don't have a valentine" was lonely. Looking at my phone over and over, wondering if any guy would ever text me—yes, it was definitely lonely.

> *When you feel alone and neglected by others—especially by a guy—the heartache can feel overwhelming.*

Time and time again I've felt alone, but through it all, I've never ever stopped loving and trusting Jesus. He made me and He knows my heart, just like He knows yours.

Give all your worries and cares to God, for he cares about you. (1 Peter 5:7 NLT)

I absolutely love everything about this verse. It's a beautiful comfort.

The moment I met Kyle, all of those lonely nights and days were worth it. I've prayed for Kyle my entire life. I can specifically remember praying for him on that cold rainy Saturday night my sophomore year of high school. The night I didn't get to go to winter formal.

How often do you pray for your future husband? It may seem like a faraway time in your life, but God wants to hear your desires and worries. Talk to Him right now.

----xo----

There was this girl named Rachel who went to my middle school. Rachel was the happiest girl. She was always smiling. I can't remember her ever gossiping about anyone, and I never heard her complain. She truly was a ray of sunshine to us all.

Rachel and I had dance in common. She took dance classes almost every day after school, and so did I. We both loved tap, jazz, ballet, and hip-hop.

Dance was one of the many creative outlets I loved using to express myself. It also was a good outlet to escape school and homework while getting in a workout. Rachel took classes at a different studio from me, but it didn't matter. We had that passion for dance in common.

Rachel came from a loving home. She had a mom, dad, and younger brother. I would go to her house for sleepovers, and in the morning her dad would make us the best chocolate chip pancakes. Rachel's family went to church and loved the Lord, which was another reason I think we hit it off right away. We were raised a lot alike.

One day we were all sitting in gym class, and our teacher was taking attendance. As soon as he was done, he announced that we were going to go outside to walk or run on the school track. We hadn't expected that lovely news, so we slowly stood up from the bleachers and started heading outside.

Before we reached the door, we heard an announcement over the loudspeaker asking Rachel to report to the front office. We all stopped and looked at her. Some kids started nervously laughing because they thought she was in trouble. I knew that wasn't true.

Rachel grabbed her backpack and headed for the front office. I asked my teacher if I could go with her. I just wanted to see what was going on. My teacher said no, but once we finished up running around the track and class was done, I headed to the office.

As I turned the corner, I saw Rachel weeping in the corner. Her mom and brother were both there holding her.

One of the office ladies pulled me aside and told me Rachel had gotten some terrible news about her dad. He had been driving back from a business trip when he was hit by a semitruck and his car flipped. He died at the scene of the crash.

I fell to the ground sobbing at the news before walking over to Rachel and what was left of her family. I could hear Rachel's mom praying. She had just lost her husband, Rachel and her brother had just lost their dad, but there they were *praying*.

I started to weep even harder.

Their level of faith in that moment didn't even make sense. The struggle and heartbreak they faced was unbearable, yet they still looked up to the heavens and prayed.

Rachel didn't come back to school for a couple of months. I spent almost every other day with her. Crying with her, just being there for her.

When she did finally come back to school, I was absolutely amazed by her attitude. People at first felt awkward around her. They weren't sure how to act or what to say. One friend came up to her and said, "Rachel, you don't deserve any of this heartache. I'm so sorry about your dad."

Rachel, being the type of person who didn't complain and who smiled through life, just said quietly, "Thank you. The pain I feel inside will never go away, but I can tell you that I still love Jesus more than anything. I'm not mad at Him. I know I will see my dad again someday."

I couldn't believe it. Rachel was facing the biggest mountain I could imagine, and she was still clinging to the hope of Jesus in her life.

Rachel's story will always stay with me. Life can be so unfair. It can bring us heartbreak that we don't deserve. The tears and the deep hurt is and always will be a part of Rachel.

But here's something that is unbelievable: she still doesn't complain. She continues to tell people that God has a plan, and she lives out her faith every day.

Do you trust that God has a plan for you? Do you believe that no matter what heartbreak you are going through right now, one day things will get better?

Do you believe that God is already orchestrating your happily ever after? You have your own unique fairy tale. It won't look like my story with Kyle, because it is designed just for *you*. Keep trusting God. Keep believing in His plan for your life.

Life is hard and we *will* face mountains. It's not easy living in a broken world. But when the trials and mountains pop up in your life, keep climbing. Climb with a smile and without complaining . . . and then climb some more! Trust that God has amazing plans waiting for you on the other side.

From Kyle

Olympic athletes train their entire lives. They discipline themselves in order to reach their goal. They prioritize their lives around their pursuit of athletic excellence. They climb and climb and climb until they reach the top.

Choosing to approach relationships God's way is not always easy, but the best things in life never are.

High school was tough for me. There were plenty of girls I was attracted to, but they didn't follow Jesus. For me that was a deal breaker. So I never had a real high school girlfriend.

One time I had to seriously look a girl in the eye and say, "Listen, I know you like me and I like you too, but I'm committed to dating only girls who pursue Jesus. My faith

> *God's way is not always easy, but the best things in life never are.*

in God is important to me. I need to be with someone who feels the same way." Boy, that was hard, especially since I had feelings for the girl.

But I took this verse to heart:

Don't develop partnerships with those who are not followers of Jesus' teachings. For what real connection can exist between righteousness and rebellion? How can light participate in darkness? (2 Cor. 6:14 VOICE)

Rebellion? Darkness? That may sound a little harsh, but dating someone is a serious thing. Dating leads to marriage. You have to be compatible, and what's more compatible than having the same beliefs about life and God?

God wants us to be with someone who will build us up and encourage our faith to grow. How is a non-Christian supposed to do that? They can't.

So while I may have liked this girl, dating her was not God's best for me. Our hearts wouldn't have matched up. I believed in Jesus and followed Him. She didn't. A difference like that affects your whole outlook on life—your choices, decisions . . . everything.

I could have tried to force us to be together, but it wouldn't have worked out in the end. Something would have to give, and it would probably be my faith in God that would take the hit. This was a mountain in my life, and I had to face it.

Was it hard saying no to her? Yes. Did my feelings for her immediately go away? No, not at all. But was it worth it? Absolutely.

I learned a great deal from that experience. I began to discipline myself about who was filling my mind and who

I even let myself begin to crush on. If a girl who wasn't a Christian turned my head, I reminded myself that our relationship could only be as friends.

I wasn't perfect at this, and there were plenty of consequences for some of my actions. But my decision to date only girls who truly loved Jesus was one of the best decisions of my life.

When I was in high school, my peers couldn't believe that I would date only Christian girls and that I was waiting for marriage to have sex. They were shocked. They definitely could not understand it, and sometimes the flak I caught from my classmates felt like a big mountain in my path.

But I didn't let their opinions get the best of me. I remained confident in who I was and in my decision.

Still, I often felt very alone.

The high school I attended only had a few Christians, and not all of them took biblical principles seriously. When kids found out about my decision to wait, they would ask me to explain in extreme detail how far was too far.

Honestly, it was ridiculous. My go-to response was, "Well, I just think about what I wouldn't want my wife doing with some other guy." That line worked pretty well.

The Bible isn't meant to keep us from fun and good things. It's not meant to put a huge hurdle in our path just for the sake of making life hard. God's Word is meant to protect us and protect our hearts. But the path can still be difficult.

Choosing to chase after God and trusting Him to bring a Christian guy into your life isn't easy. I've been there before, waiting for a Christian girl.

But I've also come down the other side of the mountain and can truly say it's worth the climb. You'll never regret your decision if you choose to complete this journey. You may feel alone at times, but remember that God is always with you.

He can help you overcome if you let Him . . . if you rest on His strength and not your own.

The world may say your happily ever after dream is impossible. They'll tell you that good guys don't exist, so stop waiting for them. The guys and girls in my class didn't want to wait. They wanted "love" now, and they settled.

Friends who aren't Christians, and maybe even some who are, might not understand you. You don't have to convince them that you're right. That's not your job. Just keep on living out your beliefs and don't compromise your values. Hold tight to God's promise that He will never leave you. Think about this passage from the Bible:

> When troubles of any kind come your way, consider it an opportunity for great joy. For you know that when your faith is tested, your endurance has a chance to grow. So let it grow, for when your endurance is fully developed, you will be perfect and complete, needing nothing. (James 1:2–4 NLT)

Trouble. Joy. At first glance those two words don't mix. But give it some time and thought. What helped me was to refocus my viewpoint. Instead of feeling lonely because I didn't have somebody to date in high school, I focused my view on the future, on what my perseverance and faith in God could give me: a beautiful girl chasing after Jesus. Someone I could fully give myself to.

Pray for your future husband in your lonely moments. Write him a letter and show it to him when you are married.

Kelsey has described to me the countless times she prayed for me when she felt alone while growing up. And I did the same for her. I prayed for her safety, for her family, for God to bless her and give her the desires of her heart. Only in heaven will we be able to see how our prayers affected our lives in those moments.

The climb is tough, but pressure-filled high school and college years don't last forever. A lifetime commitment of marriage does. Try refocusing your viewpoint. Focus on the future.

Pray about your happily ever after. Have faith you can make it there with God's help, and take the next step up the mountain.

It's worth the climb.

From Us Both

Your faith will be tested. You might fall down, but if you keep getting back up and trusting God, you can make it. Choose to be different from your friends. Stand out from the crowd.

In every fairy tale, the hero must overcome obstacles before reaching their happily ever after. Have faith and stay on course. God is with you. And trust us, the lonely times, the tears, and the climb will all be worth it when you see the view at the top!

9

Just Haven't Met You Yet

From Kelsey

If you're anything like me, you're probably already humming Michael Bublé's song "Haven't Met You Yet" after reading this chapter title. Some of you reading this book right now are already in a relationship. Others are reading this and are still single. I've been in both places, so I get it.

God created love, and ultimately God loves us more than we could ever love another human being. That's hard for me to comprehend when I think about my husband Kyle, because I love him with everything inside of me. God is love, and we should try to imitate that in our own lives. We should strive to love and to show God's love to all people.

A lot of us long for that other person who will one day walk into our lives and fill our hearts. We long for our significant other. I'm a very passionate and romantic person. I've been this way my entire life. My heart craves love. I'm a dreamer, and before meeting Kyle I dreamed of my future guy.

You see, God knows everything about me and you. He knows the desires of our hearts, even right now. He knows if you are feeling lonely. He knows if you are tired of waiting for the right guy to come into your life. He knows if you've been hurt.

God cares about your heart and your feelings.

My mom and I have always been best friends. As I was growing up, she wanted me to know that I could come to her and talk about anything and everything. So I did.

One beautiful sunny spring afternoon we were having a girls' day. My mom and I have been having these days for as long as I can remember. We go shopping, get coffee, have lunch, or go and get manicures and pedicures. Anything girly and we were there.

This particular day we had been walking up and down the pretty streets of downtown Portland. We stopped in quaint boutiques and went inside all of the major department stores. Laughing, trying on clothes, coffee in hand. Our girls' day was already a success.

We decided to take a break from shopping and eat lunch at a cute little café right in the heart of downtown. We grabbed a table outside because the sun was just too beautiful to sit inside. You see, there's nothing quite like sunshine when you live in the Pacific Northwest. It's a rare thing to even see the sun because it rains so much there.

We were all smiles as the sun's rays filled our souls.

"So, I can't believe Scott and I have been dating for almost six months." I took a bite of my salad.

My mom took a sip of her coffee. "Six months is sure exciting. Do you think you guys will ever get married?"

I almost choked on my salad. I laughed and graciously said, "No, I could never see myself actually marrying him. I mean, he's a nice guy and all . . . but I could never picture myself wanting to leave our house, leave you and Dad and the boys, to go and be married to him."

My mom nervously laughed. "Well honey, do you really think you should be dating him then? Six months is already a long time. You are both in college. It's not like I'm crazy to bring it up. What is he supposed to think if you just keep on dating him?"

I realized she was right.

Have you ever had a moment like that with your mom or with someone you are really close to? A moment where everything they just said is making complete sense, but you kind of don't want to let them know you think they are right? Yeah, that was me sitting across the table from my mom.

I leaned back in my chair and picked up my teacup. As I sipped my tea we both sat there in silence for a bit.

Eventually the words came out of my mouth. "Mom, you are so wise. You are right, we are old enough to talk about marriage . . . but I just don't ever see myself marrying him." This time we both laughed nervously.

We left the café and crossed the street to more shops. The sun felt even warmer than before, like a hug from God. The rest of our girl day was amazing. We laughed some more, and on the drive home we sang songs from Taylor Swift's *Fearless* album.

That night I was up in my room by myself. I couldn't get the lunch conversation with my mom out of my head. What in the world was I doing dating a guy who I couldn't even imagine marrying?

I grabbed my journal and wanted to write, but I couldn't. I felt so stupid. I knew that I shouldn't date a guy unless I thought I could marry him. On the other hand, how would I know if he was the right guy unless I dated him? My mind and heart were all over the place.

Three months into dating my boyfriend, I had known deep down that I was never going to marry him. But I was already too comfortable with him to break up. Remember, I'm a hopeless romantic. In other words, I loved having a boyfriend. Someone to always talk to and text with. A guy who would hold me and watch movies with me. I loved it all.

What in the world was I doing dating a guy who I couldn't even imagine marrying?

As I stared at my blank journal, I began to pray. I prayed that God would show me what to do.

Well, my boyfriend and I did celebrate our six-month anniversary. Six months turned into a year, and then a year turned into two years. I'm not kidding. My boyfriend wasn't a bad guy, I just knew deep down that he wasn't completely right for me.

At one point I actually had Michael Bublé's song "Haven't Met You Yet" as my ringtone. Yeah, I'm not very proud of that memory. My poor boyfriend.

The talks with my mom about my boyfriend continued. My dad would weigh in too, and they were both so loving and patient with me. But they would end our talks by saying, "Kels, if you aren't going to marry him and you do feel like you are called to be married one day, then what are you doing?"

It finally hit me that I needed to do something about it. Not only was I being mean to my boyfriend, but I wasn't listening to God's voice.

The last thing I wanted to do was go through a breakup. I knew I wasn't going to marry him, but I liked having a boyfriend. The truth is, I liked not being lonely. I finally put all of my comfortable, stubborn, prideful emotions aside and broke up with him.

The next few months were rough for me. I was crying all the time, and I was extremely lonely. Some nights I wanted to text him so badly, just to have someone to text. Some nights I missed him so much that I did text him. But I knew deep down he still wasn't the guy for me.

Girls, you don't always need a guy, and you certainly don't need a boyfriend just to have one. God made you so beautiful. Be confident in your singleness if you are single.

And if you are dating someone, ask yourself this: Am I willing to marry this guy? If the answer is no, then please break up with him. You are too valuable and time is too precious to waste away your days with a guy you never plan to marry.

If your mom or dad talks to you and asks how things are going in your relationship, be honest with them. Talk to God about the guy you are dating or the guy you want to date.

God already knows what you are thinking and what your heart is wrestling through. When you truly give your relationships over to God, that's when He can start to guide your steps.

> *You are too valuable and time is too precious to waste away your days with a guy you never plan to marry.*

If you're like me, then you're probably reading this thinking, "Okay, but is she saying I can't date at all until I'm ready to get married?" The answer is no, of course not. I dated several guys before meeting Kyle. Some people might disagree with me on this, but I think it's important to date to see what kind of guy you like.

Dating someone can help you figure out more of your own heart and what you actually want in a guy. But I absolutely stand by this: If you aren't planning on marrying a guy, then why stay in the relationship?

Was I lonely when I finally broke up with my boyfriend? Yes, very. But it's far better to be single than to keep dating the wrong guy.

----xo----

I met my friend Claire in college. She was a sweet and hilarious friend. We actually met each other at Starbucks.

College was fun and exciting, and everything about it was new. I was still getting used to the fact that no one was telling me to study or do my homework. I was able to create my own schedule. After class each day I would go to the track and run, or I would go take a yoga or dance class. I've always liked working out, but being away at college made me fall in love with fitness.

When I needed a little break from campus and all of the fun activities, I would go to Starbucks. The Starbucks was right next to campus, so it was safe and mostly packed with students doing the same thing as me: getting away for some study time.

It was midweek and I had a bunch of studying to do. I had several essays due the following Monday and a few other assignments to work on. I walked in to Starbucks to grab some coffee while I worked and saw there was only one open seat in the whole place. A girl was already sitting at that table, but I thought maybe she wouldn't be using the empty chair. So I ordered my drink and then asked if I could sit down.

She smiled. "Of course. Hey, my name's Claire."

I told her my name, and as we talked it turned out we both shared a loved for all things design and the store Anthropologie. We totally hit it off right away. We both agreed how college had been fun so far and it was nice to create your own schedule, but we were both desperately missing our families.

We didn't get too much studying done that day. Mostly we just laughed and told each other our stories.

Claire told me all about her boyfriend and how amazing he was. Our college was a Christian school, so I had assumed she was a Christian, and she was. But she shared with me that her boyfriend wasn't a Christian and she wasn't too happy about it.

The next time I saw Claire was at a football game. We sat by each other and had the best time taking pictures, laughing, and cheering on our team. We won that game, and the whole campus was pumped about it.

The next morning I met Claire for breakfast, and that's when she really started venting about her boyfriend. "He's everything I've ever wanted in a guy. He's sweet. He buys me flowers just because. He respects my dad, loves my mom, and is great with my little sister." She looked down at the table. "He just needs Jesus."

She went on to tell me that she had tried many times to invite him to church. She tried talking to him about God, but every time she did he became quiet and standoffish. Claire's boyfriend loved her, but he wasn't going to budge on the whole God/Christianity thing.

Claire and I remained close friends that entire year. She kept trying to get her boyfriend to be open to the idea of God, and I could tell time and time again that his resistance deeply hurt her heart.

Claire and her boyfriend are the perfect example of why so-called missionary dating is extremely hard. Girls, don't date a non-Christian. You might think you will be the girl who changes him, but it's not that easy, and he probably won't change. I know that sounds so black-and-white, but it's the truth.

If God's plan for your life is marriage, then He already has the most amazing guy picked out for you. I really can't say that enough. Kyle is everything I ever dreamed about in a guy and so much more. He is my heart, my song, my every happiness. God knew exactly what I needed and what my heart longed for when He created Kyle. I'm just so thankful God was patient with me along the journey, even when I was stubborn and impatient.

Yes, it's okay to date and have a boyfriend—depending on what your parents say, that is. You should always respect their rules on dating. But I beg you, don't have a boyfriend just to have one. Also, save yourself a lot of heartbreak and only date someone who is a Christian.

God has amazing plans for you and your future. Always protect your heart. Save not only your body but your whole heart for your future guy.

I know the waiting can be lonely, but try to fill your days with God, staying healthy, family, school, and friends. Oh, and listen to Michael Bublé's "Haven't Met You Yet" on repeat!

From Kyle

During my junior year of college I had a crush on a girl named Taylor. We took the same campus bus to class in the morning, and her dorm was across from mine. We had been flirty friends for the first few months and had just started dating.

For the first few weeks we had a great time, but she loved getting attention from all guys, not just from me. I would see her laughing loudly with a guy outside the bathroom. I would see her touch a guy's shoulder as she made her way onto the elevator.

I don't see myself as a jealous person, but deep down I could feel myself becoming jealous of Taylor and how she gave random guys the same kind of attention she gave me. It was like she couldn't turn her flirt switch off. I liked this girl, so it was pretty frustrating. I kept imagining our relationship and what it would be like if she could just figure this out.

I mentioned this to her on a dinner date one night. "Taylor, I want to talk to you about something."

"Sure, what's up?" She brushed her hair from her face and looked up at me sweetly.

"I want you to know that I'm having a lot of fun dating you."

"Oh, thank you! I'm having fun dating you too!"

"But . . . I don't really like how I sometimes feel when I'm not right beside you." I put down my fork and set my hands on the table.

"What do you mean?"

"I see you flirting with guys a lot." I just had to get the words out.

She winced, but before she could speak I said, "I don't think you do it intentionally." She took a deep breath and looked down.

"I feel like you are flirty with every guy, not just me. And that's kind of a problem."

"Kyle, I like you a lot. I can't control how other people act around me, but know that I don't like anyone else." She meant it. I could tell.

"I know that, Taylor. I just wanted to bring it up."

She actually apologized and said she would try to be intentional about how she acted around other guys. I think she understood what she was doing and how it made me feel as her boyfriend, and for the next few days I really noticed a change in her. I thought she got it.

That is, until the following week.

It was like our talk never happened. I saw her on the bus sitting really close to another guy. I saw a guy carrying her books to class. I saw a guy pulling out her chair at lunch.

I'm not kidding.

I'm all for giving someone grace, but I had the suspicion that Taylor was not the girl for me. I had a lot of red flags warning me to end things with her, but I was comfortable having a girlfriend.

So for the next few months we continued dating, and I tried to not let those flirty moments get to me. I knew she liked me. When it was just the two of us we still had a good time.

It wasn't until I came out of my dorm late one night and saw Taylor kissing another guy that it truly hit me. What was I doing? I wanted a girl who saw her worth in God, not in the approval and attention of other guys.

Even though it hurt, I'm glad God let me see that kiss. It was a huge wake-up call for me. Why was I settling?

It caused me to evaluate the whole relationship and my motives for wanting to be with her in the first place. Was I with her because I liked having a girlfriend? Did I really like *her*? Was I really pursuing God's best for my life? Or did I like the status and importance that came with dating someone?

> Guard your heart above all else,
>   for it determines the course of your life.
>   Proverbs 4:23 NLT

A romantic relationship changes you—for good or for bad. It might start off sweet and innocent, but all relationships end in one of two ways: a breakup or a marriage. The

Don't settle for someone you know **deep down** isn't the **right one** for you.

most important decision you'll make outside of choosing to follow Jesus is deciding who to marry.

Here's something I learned from my relationship with Taylor: *don't settle*. Don't settle for someone you know deep down isn't the right one for you. Don't settle for just anybody because you are lonely.

Ladies, you don't need a guy to complete you. Contrary to what every love song and movie tells you, you are complete . . . with God. He created and designed you. He formed your very heart.

If you fall in love, then God wants you to fall in love and be in a committed relationship with someone who is also following Him. That way, you can experience a true and deep kind of love, something this world doesn't understand.

And what you two care about—your values and morals—will match in a way that is beneficial to your relationship with Jesus. You'll both be chasing after Him. How can a guy who doesn't know Jesus understand the spiritual depth of your heart? He can't. A relationship like that is destined for disaster.

> *You don't need a guy to complete you.*

Boy, am I thankful I didn't settle. Kelsey is literally the girl of my dreams. The love and affirmation I get from her makes me feel like I can fly. Seriously, she makes me feel like I can do anything. She has that much belief in me. And her beauty—inside and out—literally takes my breath away.

Before I met Kelsey there were moments (a lot of them) where I doubted if she was even real. Would she ever come into my life? Had I missed her already?

But then I would pray to God, and He would always settle my heart. He would remind me that all things work in His timing, not mine. When I would try to force my plan and my timing, things would blow up in my face (case in point: Taylor).

- - - -XO- - - -

When you are trying to decide whether someone is worth dating, first ask yourself, Am I ready to date? What do my parents say? What kind of traits does this person have? Obviously, you want to date someone you are attracted to, but there's a lot more that's important than just looks.

> The Holy Spirit produces this kind of fruit in our lives: love, joy, peace, patience, kindness, goodness, faithfulness, gentleness, and self-control. (Gal. 5:22–23 NLT)

Look at those characteristics again. Love. Joy. Peace. Patience. Kindness. Goodness. Faithfulness. Gentleness. Self-control. When we live a life dedicated to God, these qualities will be evident in our lives. Does the person you want to date have any of them? How many characteristics can you see in that person? Four? One? Zero?

We can all grow and improve, but if the person you like doesn't have most of these qualities, why date him? Save yourself the time and save your heart the trouble. Wait for the guy God brings into your life who has these traits. God will show you the right person.

If you believe in Jesus, then you have the Holy Spirit living inside of you. Listen to that still small voice, especially when it comes to relationships. When you're thinking about whether or not this is the person you should date, pray.

Go to people you look up to and get wise Christian counsel. God will make it clear to you, and His opinion matters the most.

From Us Both

If we had settled for less than God's best for us, we wouldn't be writing this book. We wouldn't be together.

Maybe right now you're waiting for Mr. Right. Be patient in the waiting. Most likely you just haven't met him yet. God sees you and knows what your heart is going through. Don't get into a relationship just to have a boyfriend. Trust us, you'd rather be single than be with the wrong person.

Run to God when you're lonely. He will satisfy your heart more than a guy ever could. Trust God and pray believing.

Epilogue

TODAY WAS A FAIRY TALE

God has been chasing after you since the day you were born. He loves you more than you could ever imagine. He desires an intimate, personal relationship with you. He's a loving Father who wants to take care of you, His child.

He's seen your most treasured moments and your deepest heartbreak. He's watched you make the right decisions and also some wrong ones. He's watched you fail, but He rejoices with the greatest joy when you succeed.

He loves when you ask questions and dream. God knows everything you've ever been through. He knows your heart, and He loves you all the time.

But there's a problem: we are sinful.

God is completely holy. Sin separates us from Him.

There's good news, though: God never gives up on us.

He never stops chasing after us. He came up with an amazing way to reunite our hearts to His when we mess up and sin. He sent His Son, Jesus, to this earth to die on a cross for all our sins. The weight and sorrow of every sin was placed upon Jesus as He hung on a cross and died.

But the story doesn't end there. On the third day, Jesus came back to life. He rose from the grave, proving that death and sin have no power over Him.

Jesus triumphed over death, and He can triumph over the sins in your life if you believe in Him. When you believe in Jesus—that He rose from the dead and that He can save you—and when you ask Him to be the leader of your life, you can truly have a relationship with God. And it's a personal relationship that will last forever.

Once you do that, then the adventure of your fairy tale truly begins.

It all starts with a chase and it all ends with a chase. Our stories may look quite different, but you can be sure God will lead you to the exact plans He has for your life. God's timing is perfect. Do you trust in His perfect plans for you?

God has an amazing happily ever after planned out for you, and it's a story that could only be yours. For this story is designed just for you. Without *you*, it wouldn't exist. Are you ready to find it?

Continue to chase God. He'll show you the way.

----xo----

Remember how we started this book with "Once upon a time"? By now you know that's our story, the beginning of our happily ever after. We've shared more details of that story throughout the course of this book, but just to refresh your memory (and because we love telling the story), here's a little recap:

Once upon a time there was a boy named Kyle. He grew up in Pennsylvania. In another land far away, a girl named Kelsey grew up in Washington State. They lived 2,782 miles away from each other, yet somehow God wove their story together in a way only He could.

It was a story that would last forever.

In early 2011, Kyle was on a music tour across the West Coast. Kyle met Kelsey backstage at one of the shows in Portland, Oregon. He was immediately drawn to her. Her confidence, kindness, and beauty haunted him in the best possible way.

He knew one thing . . . he had to pursue her or he would regret it.

Kelsey thought Kyle was very attractive yet humble and kind. He made Kelsey laugh right away, and they both felt like they had known each other all of their lives. Like they had always been friends. A feeling only God brings out in two strangers.

Kyle began to pursue Kelsey.

He would drive hours to see her for only a little while before she had to catch a plane. And Kelsey would fly to Kyle's nearest shows. Endless hours of Skype dates soon followed.

They began dating. Handwritten notes, love songs, and lots of laughter colored their relationship. Memories and moments spent on both the East and West Coast filled their dating life.

They quickly fell deeply in love.

That fall, Kyle asked Kelsey's father for her hand in marriage. On a sunny autumn day in October, Kyle took Kelsey down to Main Street in Franklin, Tennessee. He got down on one knee . . . and she said yes!

That Christmas something truly special happened. Kyle and Kelsey celebrated by exchanging the letters they had written as thirteen-year-olds a decade earlier. It was the best Christmas gift either of them had ever received.

The following summer, on June 2, 2012, they continued their fairy tale as husband and wife. And since that day, life has been a beautiful, magical adventure.

And they lived happily ever after.

The End. (Or rather, to be continued . . .)

The Proposal—Kyle's Story

In October I took Kelsey on a date to Main Street in Franklin, Tennessee, one of her favorite places. At the start of our date I gave Kelsey a box I made with the words "The Map of Our Love Story" across the top. You see, Kelsey and I first met while I was on the road performing Christian music, so our love story took place in different cities across the country.

I had been planning this date for a very long time.

As we walked the street, I led Kelsey into certain shops. In each shop an employee came up and gave Kelsey a gift bag. Inside the bag was a photo of us in one of the cities we shared a memory in.

Kelsey placed the photos in the "Map of Our Love Story" box. As we walked down the street, Kelsey collected more gift bags with more photos. The photos were in chronological order and took us back to our most treasured moments.

We then came to Kelsey's favorite store, Lulu, an old brick building that housed vintage and whimsical finds. While we were inside,

Girls, you picked up this book, read our chapters, and listened to our hearts. Now it's up to you, and it comes down to a simple question: Who are you chasing?

How you answer that question will define your life. It will show you where you are headed. It will show you what you desire most. It will show you what you love most. It will show you your future.

So, who are you chasing?

Our prayer is that our love story will encourage you to believe in the unique fairy tale God has for you, the one you will find only as you chase after Jesus.

If you chase after boys, your story will be different. We're not saying it will be horrible (though it could be). What we

---

the store clerk gave Kelsey a gift bag. She opened it, and inside the bag was not a photo but a note.

It read, "Franklin, TN . . . forever starts today."

At that moment the song "Love Story" by Taylor Swift began playing outside the boutique's doors. I grabbed Kelsey's hand and led her to where our family and friends waited for us on the street. I got down on one knee and asked Kelsey to spend the rest of her life with me.

She looked down at me with wide, teary eyes and covered her mouth with her hand. She was shocked in the most beautiful way. I told her I loved her and couldn't wait to spend forever with her.

She nodded her head and said yes through tears. The biggest smile swept across my face as I stood up and kissed her. The moment felt heavenly and surreal and surprising all at once.

This was just the beginning of the story, and we couldn't wait to see where God would lead us next!

I chased after Him, and He led me to Kelsey.

---

are saying is that you will miss out on the "only God could write this" kind of love story. The kind of fairy tale we live out each and every day.

God gets all the credit for our love story. He created our hearts for each other. We are forever grateful that He is the author of our ongoing love story.

Make God your number one and have faith that He will take care of you. God created love. God is love. He knows when your heart is feeling lonely, when you wish your Prince Charming was by your side.

Never stop believing in God. Never stop dreaming and praying for your future happily ever after. God truly has the most amazing plans for you. When you chase after God, your future is full of wonder and endless possibilities.

So let the chase begin—a chase after God, that is. And trust Him with your happily ever after!

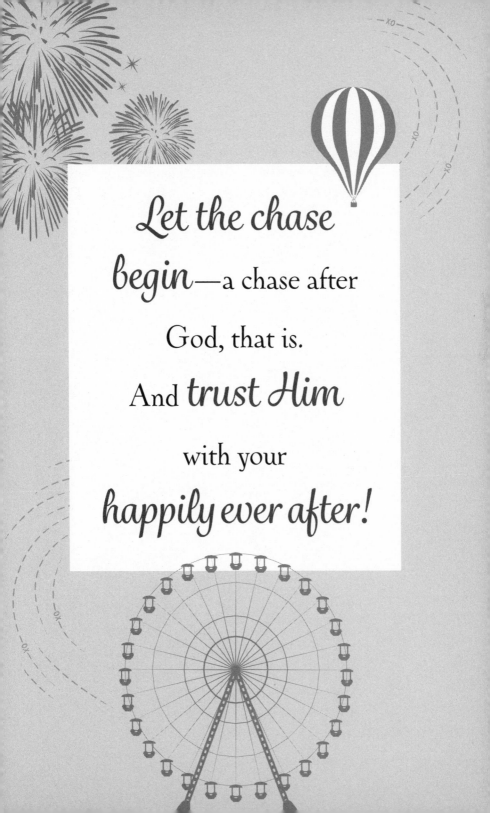

Let the chase begin—a chase after God, that is. And trust Him with your happily ever after!

Acknowledgments

If someone had told us that one day we would write a book, we would've nervously laughed. We are accidental authors. We didn't write *The Chase* because we wanted a book deal; we wrote *The Chase* because God told us we had to share our love story. We had to share the remarkable and miraculous moments only God could have orchestrated. Truly, nothing is impossible with Him.

A special thanks to the fantastic team at Revell. Your passion and dedication to this book are a dream come true. *The Chase* would not be what it is today without you all. Thank you to our dedicated editor, Jennifer Leep, and to Michele Misiak and Twila Bennett, whose creative marketing minds have made this process so fun and exciting.

Also, thanks to our amazing agent Bryan Norman and everyone at Alive Literary Agency. We are grateful for your hard work and expertise in this business. It is an honor and a privilege to be represented by you. You are the best.

A special thank-you to #1 *New York Times* bestselling author Karen Kingsbury—better known to us as Mom or mother-in-love. Thank you for showing us your secrets to writing a book. Thank you for answering our endless questions. Thank you for the coffee date where you helped us with our first ever outline. You truly are a gift. Thanks for believing in us from the beginning!

Thank you to our godly parents for showing us how to chase after God. You helped shape us into the people we are today. We are forever thankful for you! Your love, guidance, support, and prayers mean the world. We can't thank God enough for blessing us with parents who are still together and still very much in love. You are a beautiful example to us. We love you.

A big thank-you to our brothers, family, and friends. Thank you for always being there for us. We are so grateful for each and every one of you. Your friendship and love are such an encouragement. We love you all.

And the greatest thanks to God. Thank You for writing us into Your story. Every day You shower us with Your love, grace, and mercy. And for that, we can't thank You enough. Thank You for being the author of our magical love story. Our hearts are forever connected as husband and wife because of You. Thank You for leading us in this beautiful adventure we call life. We pray this book brings glory and honor to You.

Kyle Kupecky is a Christian recording artist who has toured with Lecrae, MercyMe, and Steven Curtis Chapman. His self-titled debut album released in 2014 and his Christmas album, *Snowed In*, debuted in the Top 10 on the iTunes Holiday Chart. Through his soulful pop music and public speaking along with his wife, Kyle shares his passion for Jesus with today's youth.

Kelsey Kupecky is a designer and an actress who has appeared in several faith-based films, including the Emmy-nominated *The Heart of Christmas*. She is the designer of "Possibilities," a DaySpring greeting card and gift line, with her mother, #1 *New York Times* bestselling author Karen Kingsbury.

Through acting, designing, and public speaking along with her husband, Kelsey is living out her dream of encouraging girls to chase after God, allowing Him to write their happily ever after.

Kyle and Kelsey live in Nashville, Tennessee. For more information, visit **kyleandkelsey.com**.

POSSIBILITIES™
card & gift line

Designed by Kelsey Kupecky.
Featuring quotes from #1 *New York Times*
bestselling author Karen Kingsbury.

dayspring.com